THE ORDER OF THINGS

HOW HIERARCHIES HELP US MAKE SENSE OF THE WORLD

JACKIE STRACHAN & JANE MOSELEY

ROBINSON

ROBINSON
First published in Great Britain in 2017 by Robinson

10 9 8 7 6 5 4 3 2 1

Copyright © Jackie Strachan and Jane Moseley, JMS Books, 2017

A CIP catalogue record for this book
is available from the British Library.

ISBN: 978-1-47213-990-0

Designed and typeset in Adelle
by Andrew Barron @ thextension

Printed and bound in Great Britain by Clays Ltd, St Ives plc

Papers used by Robinson are from well-managed forests
and other responsible sources.

Robinson
An imprint of
Little, Brown Book Group
Carmelite House
50 Victoria Embankment
London EC4Y 0DZ

An Hachette UK Company
www.hachette.co.uk

www.littlebrown.co.uk

Additional text by Jenni Davis, Viv Croot and Malcolm Garrard

Introduction

When does the humble list become an established hierarchy? When it places things in order of importance, seniority, authority, value, priority or status. Hierarchies create ranks, form boundaries and thereby help us to impose order on our world. They can be relatively simple, top down or bottom up, or much more complex, with branches and sub-sections. They can apply to social, cultural, musical, religious, celestial, military, corporate, environmental and biological contexts.

The orders of things in this book range far and wide from the most obvious 'I knew that' such as army and church ranks (in fact, the word hierarchy comes from the Greek word *hierarkhes* meaning sacred ruler) to the 'who knew?' (such as typography and priority at sea, among many others). Many are man-made, the result of humans imposing structure because that is what we like to do; others help us make sense of the world, some are for fun (from the omega to the alpha male), while others still occur within the natural world (the food chains of different habitats).

The world in its infinite variety is hard enough to pin down in this manner as it is and some of the pecking orders and hierarchies in this book also exist as variants according to the source, while some may be disputed by experts in the field. Hierarchies can be subjective and that is their beauty.

Society in the Edo Period

The social order in Japan during the Tokugawa or Edo period (1603–1867) under the shogunate founded by Tokugawa Ieyasu was structured around a rigid four-tier class system and was based on Confucian ideas. It was intended to create social harmony and stability, organising society in part according to the contribution made by each level to the greater whole in a *'shi-no-ko-sho'* structure. Social mobility was extremely limited. The emperor and his family held the highest status but the emperor wielded little actual power, relying heavily on the *daimyos*, the powerful nobles who were given land in return for their support. The most powerful daimyo became the *shogun*, governing the army and the country in general. During this period, the shoguns of the Tokugawa clan brought the daimyos under control.

The hierarchy was as follows, outside which were aristocrats, monastics and outcasts.

(SHI) WARRIOR CLASS OR SAMURAI

Paid for by their daimyo to control the latter's domain, they were soldiers, government administrators, tax collectors and generally wielders of great power, despite making up only a small percentage of the population.

(NO) FARMERS
The farmers fed and sustained the people and so were next in line of importance as vital members of society. This class embraced wealthy village heads, poorer tenant farmers and those who owned no land at all.

(KO) ARTISANS
As manufacturers of useful products for society, using materials produced by others but for utilitarian purposes, the artisans were next in the order. Some artisans had rich patrons while others scraped a living making simple baskets.

(SHO) MERCHANTS
Seen as the producers of nothing but instead profiteers from the work of others, merchants had the lowest social status. Some members of this class would have their own stores while others sold goods on the streets.

At the bottom of the social order were the **BURAKUMIN**, which means 'hamlet or village people'. Their occupations were considered impure or associated with death or waste (butchers, tanners, undertakers, executioners). They were stigmatised as a result. Also known as *eta* (or 'much filth'), they could be killed by members of the Samurai if they had committed a crime. Other people lived outside this system entirely and were known as *hinin*. As 'non-persons', they survived by begging, and this section of society included beggars, prostitutes and actors. The caste system along with the feudal system was abolished in 1871.

TRAVEL BAN
During the Edo period the Japanese people were forbidden to travel abroad and anyone who did so was not allowed to return. The result was a country that was virtually completely closed to the outside world until America made robust overtures in the 1850s.

Egyptian Society

Egyptian society was structured rather like their famous pyramids. This 'social pyramid' saw power held by a few at the apex, with the rest of the population descending in order of social status towards the slaves at the base. In the sky above was the pantheon of Egyptian gods led by Ra. The pharaohs were intermediaries between the gods and the people; they were the supreme leaders, exercising absolute power over their subjects. Class mobility was rare.

Pharaoh

Believed to be a god in human form, he/she made the laws and maintained order in the kingdom. Keeping the gods happy was a key part of the job.

Government officials, nobles and priests

The Vizier was the pharaoh's chief minister, second in command and sometimes serving as High Priest. He was tasked with tax collection. Outside the royal family, only nobles could hold government posts and they made local laws and generally kept order, profiting from tribute paid to the pharaoh by his subjects and donations made to the gods; priests took on the day-to-day job of pleasing the gods.

Soldiers

Their role was to protect Egypt, control unrest and supervise workers on the pyramids. Booty from battles was a perk of the job.

Scribes

Among the few literate people in Egypt, they were the record-keepers, documenting events, gifts to the gods, and numbers of soldiers or workers.

Merchants, artisans, doctors

The 'middle class', including metalworkers, painters, potters, weavers and stone carvers, who kept the country running.

Farmers, servants and construction workers

The worker ants of Egyptian society, this group fed the kingdom, ensured their superiors' every whim was met and built the pyramids and palaces. They included forced labour.

Slaves

Chattel slaves were prisoners of war or those born of slave mothers. They included bonded labourers – those who sold themselves into slavery, such as to clear a debt. The slaves worked in houses, quarries or mines and temples, but in some respects they were on a par with servants and life was often better for them than for their counterparts in other ancient civilisations.

The Elizabethan World Picture

Elizabethan England was organised according to a hierarchical system known today as the Elizabethan World Picture. A 'chain of being' linked the greatest to the least, with God at the very top of this chain, above the monarch, who ruled over all her subjects.

Queen Elizabeth
Gloriana, God's representative on earth.

Nobility
The titles of peers were bestowed by the monarch or determined by birth, passed from father to oldest son. There were around fifty noble families, usually powerful landowners. In descending order of importance: duke and duchess, marquis and marchioness, earl and countess, viscount and viscountess, baron and baroness. (Archbishops held the same rank as dukes and bishops the same as earls.)

Gentry
A class made up of, in descending order of importance, knights, squires and gentlemen. Also landowners on a smaller scale, they were often very wealthy.

Yeomanry
A kind of middle class that included farmers who owned or worked small parcels of land, merchants, tradesmen and shopkeepers.

Peasants, labourers and servants
Non-land owning.

The poor, beggars and people unable to work
With the first rumblings of a rudimentary welfare system, the Poor Law made the parishes responsible for their poor, who were in turn classified as:

• Helpless poor, including the old, sick and disabled.

• Able-bodied poor, who wanted to work but were unemployed.

• Rogues and vagabonds, able-bodied but more inclined to steal or beg than work.

4

The Ant Colony

Ants are 'eusocial' creatures, meaning that they have a developed social structure and live in colonies with a strict caste system. Their life cycle involves four developmental stages: egg, larva, pupa and adult, and it is during the larval stage that an ant's future is determined. Male ants have just one job to perform – to mate. The best-nourished female larvae will grow wings and become queens, whereas those who don't receive much TLC from the other ants become workers or soldiers. Additional worker castes (e.g. media or super soldiers) exist in some ant species such as leaf cutters. Only the queen reproduces and most of her offspring become workers and soldiers who collect food, protect the colony and raise the young.

Queen
She may be top ant but she doesn't order the other ants about, her sole role is to produce offspring. Depending on the species, a colony may have just one or multiple queens.

Male
Born to mate with as many queens as possible and survive for the mating season only. A brief but very busy life.

Normal-sized worker
Worker ants are female and usually sterile; they forage, and build and defend the nest. A life of toil.

Soldier
Larger workers (may be equipped with sword-like jaws) that defend the colony. The Lara Crofts of the ant world.

Nurse
Smaller workers who care for the larvae. Busy little bees but not literally.

5   The Hochadel

Until the *de facto* abolition of family titles in 1919 by the Weimar Republic, Germany had an aristocracy that had flourished from the earliest times of the Holy Roman Empire, through the German Confederation that replaced it and into the German Empire. The Uradel ('original nobility') included families whose rank dated back to the fourteenth century or earlier, while the Briefadel ('lettered nobility') were a slightly more *arriviste* cadre whose title rested on letters patent granted in more recent times; these included a large number of the bourgeoisie made good, including the likes of literary Wunderkind Goethe, who was ennobled only in 1782 by Duke Carl August of Saxe-Weimar (making his full name Johann Wolfgang *von* Goethe). The Hochadel ('high nobility') were those of royal, princely or ducal blood, and these held precedence over all other ranks.

KAISER/KAISERIN
Emperor/Empress.

KÖNIG/KÖNIGIN
King/Queen.

KURFÜRST/KURFÜRSTIN
Prince-elector/electress. A prince of the Holy Roman Empire who had the right to take part in electing the emperor.

ERZHERZOG/ERZHERZOGIN
Archduke/duchess. Governed an archduchy.

GROSSHERZOG/GROSSHERZOGIN
Grand duke/duchess. Originally a ruler governing a state that was not large enough to be a kingdom, after the title 'duke' lost prestige, having been granted to the rulers of relatively small regions.

GROSSFÜRST/GROSSFÜRSTIN
Grand prince/princess. Originally a ruler over several tribes or a feudal overlord of other nobles.

HERZOG/HERZOGIN
Duke/duchess.

PFALZGRAF/PFALZGRÄFIN
Count/countess palatine. From the Latin comes *palatinus*, 'count of the palace'.

MARKGRAF/MARKGRÄFIN
Margrave/margravine. A marquess; originally a count or earl protecting a march (a border province).

LANDGRAF/LANDGRÄFIN
Landgrave/landgravine. A title entrenched in German feudal law, which allowed for individuals and city-states that were under the direct authority of the Holy Roman Emperor rather than a local ruler.

REICHSFÜRST/REICHSFÜRSTIN
Prince/princess of the empire. A *princeps imperii* was a prince whose title had been recognised by the Holy Roman Emperor.

REICHSGRAF/REICHSGRÄFIN
Count/countess of the empire. Originally a count of the Holy Roman Empire.

BURGGRAF/BURGGRÄFIN
Burgrave/burgravine. Originally a twelfth–thirteenth-century governor of the castle that defended a city or town and its immediate environs.

ALTGRAF/ALTGRÄFIN
Altgrave/Altgravine. A title used by the counts of Lower Salm to distinguish themselves from the counts of Upper Salm, who were the cadet branch of the family.

REICHSFREIHERR/REICHSFREIFRAU
Baron/baroness of the empire – once again, a title recognised by the Holy Roman Emperor.

HERR
Lord.

REICHSRITTER
Imperial knight. These were minor nobility whose estates were held as tenants of the crown.

Royal Lines of Succession

Historically, the question of who steps up when a monarch dies has often proved a bone of contention, leading to civil and even international wars. These days, however, it is far less chaotic. In the UK, home to what is generally acknowledged as the world's most famous monarchy, there are one hundred names on the royal line of succession list. But it is constantly evolving as new marriages are made and new babies (aka claimants) are born – and the rules changed radically when the Succession to the Crown Bill 2013 was introduced, putting an end to a centuries-old tradition of male primogeniture, whereby boys precede their elder sisters (if there are elder sisters) in the line.

The line directly descended from Queen Elizabeth II currently stands as follows:

1 Prince Charles (Queen's eldest son)

2 Prince William (Prince Charles's elder son)

3 Prince George (Prince William's son)

4 Princess Charlotte (Prince William's daughter)

5 Prince Henry, or Harry (Prince Charles's younger son)

6 Prince Andrew (Queen's second son)

7 Princess Beatrice (Prince Andrew's elder daughter)

8 Princess Eugenie (Prince Andrew's younger daughter)

9 Prince Edward (Queen's youngest son)

10 James, Viscount Severn (Prince Edward's son)

11 Lady Louise Windsor (Prince Edward's daughter)

12 Princess Anne (Queen's daughter)

13 Peter Phillips (Princess Anne's son)

14 Savannah Phillips (Peter Phillips's daughter)

15 Isla Phillips (Peter Phillips's daughter)

16 Zara Tindall (Princess Anne's daughter)

17 Mia Grace Tindall (Zara Tindall's daughter)

WE ARE NOT AMUSED

When English king Henry I's son and heir, William, died in a shipwreck in 1120, Henry made the unprecedented move of nominating his only other legitimate child, his daughter, Matilda, as his new heir. But despite Henry making his court swear an oath of loyalty to Matilda and her successors, it was Matilda's cousin, Stephen, who acceded, with their support, on Henry's death. Matilda was not amused, and the result was a civil war, known as the Anarchy, that lasted nearly twenty years.

Most European royal houses have similarly adopted primogeniture (first-born inherits), although Spain and Monaco currently still use male-preference primogeniture. An unusual exception is Liechtenstein, which has a system of agnatic primogeniture – in the absence of any children, inheritance passes to male collateral relatives; women only get a look-in if there is not one single male heir to be found.

In France, where the 'absolute' monarchy came to a violent end with the Revolution and was reinvented as a constitutional monarchy with the Napoleonic emperors (which itself came to an end with the death of Empress Eugénie in 1920), there are currently two 'pretenders' to the throne, should it ever be reinstated – Louis Alphonse, Duke of Anjou, and Henri d'Orléans, Count of Paris, Duke of France.

Peers of the Realm

There are five ranks in the English hereditary peerage, all conferred by the monarch. A peer of the realm may hold one or more titles from within these five ranks at the same time. The system evolved in feudal times, when men who swore an oath of loyalty to the monarch received protection or property in return. Modern peerages are created by letters patent under the Great Seal – the seal represents the sovereign's authority – rather than by the more dashing fastening of a ceremonial sword to the wearer's belt or girdle (cincture), as was the case for dukes and earls until 1615. Peerages in the top five ranks are hereditary. Most are passed on through the male line, but some pass on through heirs-general, meaning they can pass down the female line.

Within each rank, precedent is established by the date the peerage was created: the earlier the date, the more senior the title-bearer.

FIRST RANK

DUKE

Derives from the Latin *dux* meaning leader, and originally only kings were also dukes until kings began conferring dukedoms on their sons and favourites.

The first English duke was created in 1337, when Edward III conferred the Dukedom of Cornwall on his son Edward of Woodstock, the Black Prince.

Originally created by cincture, then by letters patent under the Great Seal.

The first duke not a member of the royal family was Sir William de Pole, Marquess of Suffolk, who was made Duke of Suffolk in 1448.

Formal written address: The Most Noble Duke of . . .

Spoken address: Your Grace/His Grace.

Any military, ecclesiastical or ambassadorial rank is given first: for example, Major-General, the Duke of . . .

ROYAL DUKES

A prince of royal blood is created duke either on his coming of age or marriage. Current royal dukes are Cambridge (Prince William), York (Prince Andrew), Gloucester (Prince

Richard, grandson of George V) and Kent (Prince Edward, grandson of George V).

DUCHESS
The wife of a duke.

Formal written address: The Most Noble Duchess of . . .

Spoken address: Your Grace/Her Grace.

PUT UP YOUR DUKES
Some dukedoms can pass through the female line, in which case the title duke is retained. Queen Elizabeth II is also the Duke of Lancaster, as the title is always held by the reigning monarch.

SECOND RANK

MARQUESS/MARQUIS
A foreign import, introduced in 1385 by Richard II. It was never popular, especially among earls, whose status it usurped, and is little used now; the last new marquess to be conferred was in 1926.

The first marquess was Robert de Vere, Earl of Oxford, who was made Marquess of Dublin in 1385.

Conferred by letters patent under the Great Seal.

Formal written address: The Marquess of . . .

Spoken address: Your Lordship.

Any military, ecclesiastical or ambassadorial rank is given first: for example, Major-General, the Marquess of . . .

MARCHIONESS
The wife of a marquess.

Formal written address: The Marchioness of . . .

Spoken address: Your Ladyship.

THIRD RANK

EARL
Introduced to England by Danish king Canute (c 994–1036); made hereditary under Norman rule.

Originally created by cincture, then by letters patent under the Great Seal.

Formal written address: The Right Hon, the Earl of ... (unless you are royal, in which case it is HRH, the Earl of ...).

Spoken address: Lord (name of earldom).

Any military, ecclesiastical or ambassadorial rank is given first: for example, Major-General, the Earl of ...

COUNTESS
The wife of an earl.

The female inheritor of an earldom.

Formal written address: The Right Hon, Countess of ... (unless you are royal, in which case it is HRH, the Countess of ...).

Spoken address: Lady (name of earldom).

FOURTH RANK

VISCOUNT
The name derives from the Latin *vicecomes,* meaning aide or lieutenant of a count.

The first viscount was created in 1440 by Henry VI, king of both England and France, who elevated John, 6th Baron Beaumont to the title of Viscount Beaumont of England and Viscount Beaumont of France.

The title did not become popular until the seventeenth century.

Conferred by letters patent under the Great Seal.

Formal written address: The Right Hon, the Viscount ...

Spoken address: Lord (name of viscountcy).

Any military, ecclesiastical or ambassadorial rank is given first: for example, Major-General, Viscount ...

VISCOUNTESS
The wife of a viscount.

Formal written address: The Right Hon, the Viscountess ...

Spoken address: Lady (name of viscountcy).

FIFTH RANK

BARON

A baron was originally a landowning tenant of the monarch. They were summoned by Royal writ to attend Counsel or Parliament, like a kind of early House of Lords.

In 1387, Richard II created the first baron by letters patent under the Great Seal. This was John Beauchamp de Holt, Baron Kidderminster.

Formal written address: Lord (name of barony).

Spoken address: Lord (name of barony).

Any military, ecclesiastical or ambassadorial rank is given first: for example, Major-General, Lord (name of barony) …

BARONESS

The wife of a baron.

A baroness in her own right.

Formal written address: Lady (name of barony).

Spoken address: Lady (name of barony).

COURTESY TITLE

The son and heir apparent of a duke, marquess or earl may use one of his father's titles as long as it is of a lesser grade. First sons of marquesses and earls take the courtesy title of viscount.

8 Freemasons

An international and historically secret society established to provide mutual help and fellowship among its members, who meet as equals, whatever their background. The first recorded initiation of a freemason is dated 16 October 1646, but the society's origins are thought to lie with a guild of stonemasons established in the late eleventh century in Europe. Skilled masons were highly sought after, and, unlike serfs, were able to travel around practising their art – hence, they were 'free' masons. Fraternity 'lodges' were formed, and in 1717 four London lodges met at an alehouse, the Goose and the Gridiron, united and declared themselves a Grand Lodge – the world's first – with a Grand Master.

The Freemasons are famed for their elaborate ceremonies at which new members are admitted and for the annual installation of the Master and officers of the Lodge. Collar 'jewels' are worn to denote the rank of the wearer, which is also indicated by where they sit in the Lodge. There are two levels of officer: progressive (who move up a rank each year) and non-progressive.

PROGRESSIVE OFFICERS

WORSHIPFUL MASTER
The highest honour a Lodge can bestow. The Master sits in the east end of the Lodge and usually conducts the Lodge ceremonies.

SENIOR AND JUNIOR WARDEN
Both assist the Master in running the Lodge. The Senior Warden sits opposite the Master at the west end of the Lodge, and the Junior Warden at the south.

SENIOR AND JUNIOR DEACON
The deacons accompany the candidates during the ceremonies of the Three Degrees (Entered Apprentice, Fellow Craft, Master Mason). They each carry a wand as a badge of office.

INNER GUARD
Sits just inside the door of the Lodge to check that only qualified persons enter.

STEWARD
Main function is to assist at the post-meeting dinner.

IMMEDIATE PAST MASTER (IPM)
Sits on the left of the Worshipful Master and acts as his guide and support.

CHAPLAIN
Leads the prayers at the beginning and end of each meeting.

TREASURER
Responsible for the Lodge finances and for recommending the amount of the annual subscription.

SECRETARY
Deals with the administration of the Lodge, including organising meetings and distributing the agenda.

DIRECTOR OF CEREMONIES (DC)
Oversees the ceremonies, including rehearsals, and ensures that the ceremonies are conducted with decorum.

ALMONER
The Lodge welfare officer, with an in-depth knowledge of resources for those in need.

CHARITY STEWARD
Organises charity collections and makes suggestions as to which charities to support.

ASSISTANT DIRECTOR OF CEREMONIES (ADC)
As the name suggests, the ADC assists the DC...

ASSISTANT SECRETARY
...while the Assistant Secretary assists the Secretary.

TYLER
Usually stationed outside to guard the Lodge entrance and prevent any unwanted people from entering. Historically, handshakes or 'tokens' and passwords were used to identify legitimate visitors.

ORGANIST
Provides the music for meetings and ceremonies.

ROLLED-UP TROUSER LEG – FACT OR FICTION?
In some lodges one-act plays are staged during initiation and progression to a higher level, and postulant masons roll up their trouser leg to demonstrate they are free men, and not wearing a shackle.

Who Eats Whom?

Who preys on whom in the natural order of things? Few food chains are exclusive – although often specialised in their diets, most creatures consume more than one type of food, hence individual food chains interrelate to form a complex food web.

PRIMARY PRODUCERS – AUTOTROPHS
Self-sufficient organisms that make their own nutrients, such as plants through photosynthesis and bacteria through chemosynthesis.

PRIMARY CONSUMERS – HERBIVORES
Animals that eat primary producers.

SECONDARY CONSUMERS – PRIMARY CARNIVORES
Carnivores that eat herbivores.

TERTIARY CONSUMERS – SECONDARY CARNIVORES
Large carnivores that eat primary carnivores. They are usually larger and faster than the primary carnivores.

QUATERNARY CONSUMERS – APEX PREDATORS
They have no natural predators other than man.
Lions, sharks, polar bears …

In charge of waste disposal, **DECOMPOSERS AND DETRITIVORES** complete the cycle, feeding on and breaking down organic material turning it into nutrients to return to the soil and nourish plants.

- Decomposers: organisms such as fungi and bacteria.
- Detritivores: animals such as worms and dung beetles.

EXAMPLES OF FOOD CHAINS

MARINE FOOD CHAIN
phytoplankton (tiny organisms floating in the sea)
zooplankton (e.g. krill)
squid
tuna
shark

DESERT FOOD CHAIN
cactus fruit
mouse
snake
lizard
hawk

The Male of the Species

An unscientific look at the pecking order that operates loosely in the human male 'pack'.

α **ALPHA MALE**
Mr Big Guy, confident, charismatic, self-assured, dominant, driven, at ease socially, the life and soul of a party; natural leader, captain of industry, star of the soccer team, very successful with women.

β **BETA MALE**
Mr Nice Guy, Mr Normal, less socially confident and more submissive than Alphas, with whom he tends to spend time, more reserved and moderate; good middle manager and good friend for women.

γ **GAMMA MALE**
Mr My-Own-Guy, self-reliant, self-motivated, follows his own path, doesn't hang around Alpha or Beta males; thinkers, artists and hipsters, successful with women.

δ **DELTA MALE**
Mr Introvert, private, withdrawn, subordinate, crowd-pleasing; service provider, mostly unsuccessful with women.

σ **SIGMA MALE**
Mr Lone Wolf, outrider and outsider in society, quiet but not shy, unconventionally clever, an introverted Alpha; surprisingly successful with women.

ω **OMEGA MALE**
Mr Low Status, lacking in drive, socially awkward, shirks responsibility; often rejected by women. Omega is the twenty-fourth and final letter of the Greek alphabet.

Taxonomy of the Living World

Philosopher, scientist and all-round intellectual Aristotle was the first to attempt to classify organisms in the fourth century BC. He classified plants and animals according to their similarities, grouping together those animals that lived on land, those in water and those in the air. But it was eighteenth-century Swedish botanist Carl Linnaeus who really blazed a trail for taxonomy, and his system is still in use today, albeit with some changes. As methods for scientific investigation improve and new discoveries are made it seems that nothing is set entirely in stone – some classifications are even now hotly disputed – and his system could be tweaked again or even reinvented further down the line.

Here are two basic examples from the Linnaean system.

	Cat	Rose
Domain	Eukarya	Eukarya
Kingdom	Animalia	Plantae
Phylum	Chordata	Magnoliophyta
Class	Mammalia	Magnoliopsida
Order	Carnivora	Rosales
Family	Felidae	Rosaceae
Genus	Felis	Rosoideae
Species	Felis catus	Rosa L.

In *Rosa L.* above, 'L' is for Linnaeus who described it in his *Species Plantarum* published in 1753. The binomial system gives species a two-part Latin name: genus (e.g. *Homo*) + species (e.g. *sapiens*). Some of the classifications can be divided further, into subphylum and infraphylum, and so on.

DOMAINS

American microbiologist Carl Woese proposed the three-domain system in 1977 to differentiate between cellular life forms: archaea, bacteria and eukarya. Both archaea and bacteria comprise simple single-celled microorganisms with no distinct nucleus, while eukarya are advanced complex organisms, with cells that possess clearly defined nuclei, including plants and animals. Eukarya subdivides into kingdoms.

Mohs Scale of Mineral Hardness

A ten-point scale of the hardness of minerals, based on one mineral's capacity to scratch a softer material so that the scratches can be seen by the naked eye. All minerals can be measured against the Mohs scale and assigned a hardness. For example, gold comes in on the scale at 2.5–3. Minerals can also measure below 1 or be off the scale beyond 10.

Mohs hardness	Mineral	Chemical Formula
1	Talc	$Mg_3Si_4O_{10}(OH)_2$
2	Gypsum	$CaSO_4 \cdot 2H_2O$
3	Calcite	$CaCO_3$
4	Fluorite	CaF_2
5	Apatite	$Ca_5(PO_4)_3(OH-,Cl-,F-)$
6	Orthoclase Feldspar	$KAlSi_3O_8$
7	Quartz	SiO_2
8	Topaz	$Al_2SiO_4(OH-,F-)_2$
9	Corundum	Al_2O_3
10	Diamond	C

The scale was devised in 1812 by Friedrich Mohs, a German geologist and mineralogist, while he was working for Archduke Johann of Austria.

13   Merino Wool

Merino wool is graded according to the diameter of the fibre, crimp, yield, colour and staple strength, but the fineness is the most important factor in determining its quality and price. The wool is most prized as it is so fine, soft and comfortable against the skin. Its microscopic diameter is about one-third to one-tenth the thickness of human hair. Fine yarns are used for fabrics and knitting yarns, whereas medium wool is used in woven cloths, knitting yarns and furnishings. Broad wool is more durable and therefore used to make carpets and furnishings. The Micron system uses microns (equal to 1/1,000 of a millimetre or 1/1,000,000 of a metre) to measure the diameter of a wool fibre.

Merino wool grades

Grade	Micron
Extra fine	14.5 and finer
Ultra fine	14.6–15.5
Super fine	15.6–18.5
Fine	18.6–20.5
Medium	20.6–22.5
Broad	over 22.6

14   The pH Scale

The pH scale indicates how acidic or alkaline a substance is. It is a measure of the concentration of hydrogen (H) ions compared to that in distilled water. The scale ranges from 0 to 14. A pH of 7 is neutral. Pure water is neutral. A pH less than 7 is acidic. A pH greater than 7 is alkaline. The scale works logarithmically, so that each whole value below or above pH 7 is ten times more acidic or alkali than the next one up (or down). So, a substance rated pH 3 is ten times more acidic than one rated pH 4, and 100 times more than pH 5. The scale was first devised in 1909 by Danish chemist Søren Sørensen (1868–1939) – while working for the Carlsberg Institute researching the chemistry of their beer – and revised in 1924. Examples are given below for each level.

HIGHLY ACIDIC

1   battery acid

2   lemon juice

3   vinegar

4   tomatoes

5   black coffee

6   milk

7   distilled water

8   sea water

9   baking soda

10   mild detergent

11   ammonia

12   soapy water

13   bleach

HIGHLY ALKALINE   14   drain cleaner

PERSONAL PH
*Healthy human skin is fairly acidic with a pH of between
4 and 6, helping it to fight off unwanted bacteria and fungi.*

The Scoville Scale

The heat of chillies is measured in SHUs (Scoville Heat Units) – the higher the number, the hotter the chilli. The Scoville Unit is named for Wilbur Scoville, an American pharmacist who in 1912 devised a method of measuring the comparative heat of various chilli peppers. Chillies, or the capsaicin they contained, were an important pharmaceutical ingredient.

The Scoville Method is based on dilution. One grain (65 milligrams) of ground chilli is left overnight in 100cc of alcohol. The solution is then progressively diluted with sugar water. Trained tasters sample the solution at each dilution, until the heat of the chilli can no longer be detected. Each dilution equals one SHU (Scoville Heat Unit); the stronger the chilli, the more dilutions needed to reduce it to zero – the uber-eyewatering Carolina Reaper needs to be diluted as many as 2.2 million times to get to zero. Pure capsaicin measures 16,000,000 on the Scoville scale.

	Chilli/Pepper	SHU
ZERO HEAT	Bell Pepper	0
	Peperoncini, Cherry Pepper	100–500
	Paprika	100–900
	Poblano, Pepperdew	1000–4000
	Jalapeno	3,500–10,000
	Serrano	10,000–23,000
	Cayenne, Tabasco	30,000–50,000
	Piri piri	50,000–100,000
	Bird's Eye Chilli	100,000–225,000
	Scotch bonnet	100,000–350,000
	Red Savina habanero	350,000–580,000
	Ghost pepper (Bhut Jolokia)	855,000–2,200,000
	Trinidad Moruga Scorpion	1,200,000–2,000,000
	Naga Viper	1,382,110–2,000,000
EYEWATERING!	Carolina Reaper	1,600,000–2,200,000

Where the figures given have a wide range it is because the heat varies from individual pepper to pepper.

16   The Kitchen Brigade

A military unit in microcosm, it may come as no surprise to learn that the chain of command in a professional kitchen, as developed by Auguste Escoffier in the late nineteenth century, was based on his experience of the French army. Variations can be seen in the professional kitchens of large and small establishments across the world, with some roles being combined where a smaller team is employed. The hierarchy makes the role and authority of each member very clear. Kitchens have been compared to fields of battle . . .

Chef de cuisine
(kitchen chief)

The 'kitchen chief' is in overall charge of the kitchen, supervising staff, including apprentices, hygiene, menus, recipes and the procurement of raw ingredients. Also known in some restaurants as the executive chef and in larger establishments this is a separate role at the very top of the hierarchy.

Sous-chef de cuisine
(deputy)

Reports to the chef de cuisine for the management of the kitchen.

Chef de partie
(senior chef)

Manages a station in the kitchen where particular dishes are prepared.

Cuisinier/Cuisinier de partie (cook)

Usually prepares specific dishes in a station in an independent role.

Commis
(junior cook)

Also works in a specific station and reports to the chef de partie.

Apprenti(e)
(apprentice)

Helps with preparation and cleaning in all the various stations in order to gain practical experience while studying.

Plongeur
(dishwasher)

Washes dishes and utensils but may also help with food preparation. In larger kitchens there is also a dedicated pot and pan washer (marmiton).

Aboyeur (announcer/ expediter)

Charged with accepting orders from the restaurant and relaying them to the appropriate kitchen station.

Tournand
(spare hand)

Moves around helping at various stations.

Communard
(staff cook)

Prepares the meals served to the staff, also known as the family meal.

| **Garçon de cuisine** (kitchen boy) | Supports the team in larger establishments, helping with preparation and other duties. |

THE SPECIALISTS

Pâtissier (pastry cook): Prepares baked items, desserts and sweets (and sometimes breads). This role can also be broken down into other areas of specialisation:

• **Boulanger** (baker): Prepares unsweetened doughs.

• **Confiseur** (confectioner): Prepares candies and petit fours.

• **Glacier** (ice cream maker): Prepares cold and frozen desserts.

• **Décorateur:** Responsible for showpieces and special cakes.

Boucher (butcher): Butchers meat, poultry and sometimes fish.

Saucier (sauce maker/sauté cook): Prepares sauces and sautéed items. A key position.

Rôtisseur (roast cook): In charge of the team that cooks roasts and deep-fried dishes.

Grillardin (grill cook): Prepares grilled foods.

Friturier (fry cook): Prepares fried foods in place of the rôtisseur.

Poissonnier (fish cook): Prepares fish and seafood dishes.

Entremetier (entrée preparer): A combination of potager and legumier, prepares vegetable soups and stocks (and other vegetable dishes).

• **Potager** (soup cook): Prepares soups and reports to the entremetier.

• **Legumier** (vegetable cook): Prepares vegetable dishes and also reports to the entremetier.

Garde manger (pantry or cold-foods chef): In charge of cold foods, hors d'oeuvres, appetisers, buffets and all kinds of charcuterie items.

Wine Classification

There have been many attempts at classifying wine over the ages – by country or region of origin, by grape variety, by vinification method, by vintage, even by sweetness, while most restaurant menus list bottles more prosaically by colour and price. The European Union usually classifies wine made in its member countries by *appellation*, a French term that indicates the wine's region of origin and guarantees standards of grape variety used and winemaking techniques. The top four wine-producing countries in the EU are France, Italy, Spain and Germany. From the humblest to the poshest, their individual classification systems are as follows:

FRANCE

VSIG *(vin sans indication géographique)*/**Vin de France**
Replaces the old *Vin de Table* (table wine) designation. The grape variety and even year may be specified, but the region is not given. Simple wines for everyday drinking.

IGP *(indication géographique protégée)*
Wine with a stated geographical origin but made to less strict specifications than AOC/AOP. It is starting to replace the old *Vins de Pays* (country wine) designation, although this is still also used.

AOP *(appellation d'origine protégée)*/ **AOC** *(appellation d'origine contrôlée)*
AOP is a European designation for the top-quality wines. Wines made in specific regions, from particular grape varieties and conforming to strict regulations. The French equivalent is AOC (*appellation d'origine contrôlée*), which is still also used, or AC (*appellation contrôlée*).

THE LETTERS OF THE LAW
Wines previously categorised as VDQS (vin délimité de qualité supérieure) *must now either qualify as AOP/AOC or be downgraded to IGP.*

Deutscher Tafelwein (German table wine)
A wine mostly for local consumption that must comply with only a few restrictions. A lesser-quality wine that may also be used for blending.

Deutscher Landwein (German country wine)
A minimum of 0.5% more alcohol than Tafelwein; produced from one of a number of specified districts.

Qualitätswein bestimmter Anbaugebiete (QbA)
A quality wine from a specific region or appellation that must comply with regulations (must be from a single wine-growing region, using approved grape varieties). May be chaptalised (sugar is added before fermentation to increase the alcohol).

Prädikatswein (previously Qualitätswein mit Prädikat, QmP)
Wines of special distinction (not chaptalised) divided into several categories, with increasing levels of sugar as follows:

Kabinett
Usually a light wine. Dry, medium-dry, or sweet.

Spätlese (late harvest)
A superior-quality wine and more intense in flavour, made from grapes picked after the normal harvest. Dry, medium-dry or sweeter.

Auslese (select harvest)
Often similar to a dessert wine although it can be dry, medium-dry or sweet.

Beerenauslese (berry selection)
Rich, sweet dessert wines.

Eiswein (ice wine)
Made from grapes that have frozen while still on the vine and that may also have been affected by the *botrytis* fungus (noble rot). Very concentrated sweet wines with high acidity. Made in small amounts only as Eiswein is reliant on the right weather conditions and the grapes being picked at the right moment. Eiswein durch Technik!

Trockenbeerenauslese (dry berries selection)
From specially selected grapes picked when they have dried on the vine almost to raisins. Rich, sweet and luscious.

ITALY

VdT (vino da tavola)

Table wine. Cheap, simple local wines for local consumption.

IGT (indicazione geografica tipica)

Wine that is typical of its geographical region (the focus is not on grape variety). Usually fairly basic but reasonable wines to be drunk young. Most of the good-quality 'Super Tuscans' are in this category – red wines from Tuscany that do not adhere to the strict DOC or DOCG rules.

DOC (denominazione di origine controllata)

Made according to specific rules (over three hundred appellations all with their own rules). DOCs of consistently high quality are promoted to DOCG.

DOCG (denominazione di origine controllata e garantita)

Guaranteed to be made according to strict rules to a very high standard, from permitted grape varieties. Sealed with a numbered governmental stamp across the cork as a guarantee of authenticity.

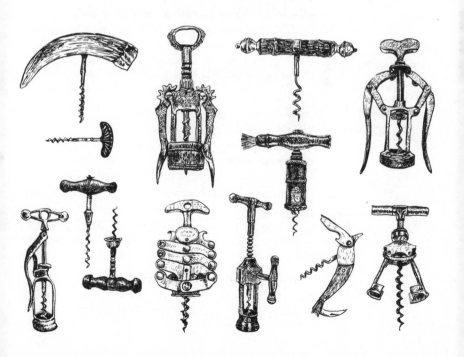

SPAIN

VdM (vino de mesa)
Table wine that does not specify a region or grape variety.

VdlT (vino de la tierra)
'Wine of the land'. Regional wines that are not produced in DO-designated areas and do not follow strict regulations. They can offer good quality and value for money.

VCIG (vinos de calidad con indicación geográfica)
Quality wines with geographical indication. After five years at this level, a VCIG wine may apply for DO status.

DO (denomination de origen)
Designation of origin. Good-quality wines from over sixty different designated regions that must comply with strict standards. Over half the total wine-growing area of Spain produces DO wines.

DO Pago (vino de pago)
Single-estate wines with an excellent reputation but unable to claim DO status, e.g. due to being outside the catchment area. Allowed to set their own regulations for production.

DOC/DOCa (denominación de origen calificada)
Appellation of origin. The most strict classification producing the highest-quality Spanish wines. To date only the Rioja and Priorat (in Catalonia where the designation is DOQ) regions have this classification.

WINE AGEING CLASSIFICATION

Joven – wines under fifteen months old.
Crianza – aged for at least two years.
Reserva – aged for at least three years.
Gran Reserva – aged for at least five years.

Champagne Bottles

A standard Champagne bottle contains 75cl of Champagne, or approximately six to eight glasses of Champagne, depending on the size of your glass or flute. Other sizes are available with increasingly exotic names, but anything above a Nebuchadnezzar is usually made to order for special occasions.

Quart	20cl	quarter standard bottle
Demie	37.5cl	half standard bottle
Standard	75cl	
Magnum	150cl	2 standard bottles
Jeroboam	300cl	4 standard bottles
Rehoboam	450cl	6 standard bottles
Methuselah	600cl	8 standard bottles
Salmanazar	900cl	12 standard bottles
Balthazar	1200cl	16 standard bottles
Nebuchadnezzar	1500cl	20 standard bottles

SIZE MATTERS
The smaller the bottle, the quicker the champagne inside it will age. This is because the neck size for a quart, demie, standard or magnum of champagne is the same, so the air-to-wine ratio is smaller in a magnum than in, say, a demie, so champagne ages more slowly in a bigger bottle.

Special occasion bottles

Solomon	1800cl	24 standard bottles
Sovereign	2625cl	35 standard bottles*
Primat or Goliath	2700cl	36 standard bottles
Melchizedek	3000cl	40 standard bottles

*Made just once by Taittinger in 1988 for the launch of the world's then biggest cruise ship *The Sovereign of the Seas*.

BIBLICAL BUBBLES
Most bottles larger than a magnum are named for Old Testament kings of Israel – Balthazar, for example, was one of the three Magi. No one really knows why the bottles are so named, although there is much speculation. They were all men of worth, standing and importance; perhaps the champagne makers wanted to confer some gravitas on their product.

Michelin Stars

In 1900 the Michelin tyre company published its first guidebook to encourage people to travel around France, a book with a blue cover given free to motorists with information on garages, accommodation and meals. In 1926 the company sent anonymous reviewers to try out various of the country's restaurants and submit their feedback and in that year the first star was awarded. The three-star system was inaugurated five years later. The anonymity and meticulous documentation continue today, and after detailed reports are carefully reviewed and discussed in lengthy meetings between inspectors and the guide's editors, stars are awarded, retained or lost.

Bib Gourmands restaurants were introduced in 1997 – and are also listed in the Michelin guidebooks. 'Bib' comes from the 'Michelin Man' logo, known as 'Bibendum'. The restaurants are listed in the standard *Michelin Guides* (the famous *Guides Rouges*/Red Guides) and in their own dedicated guide, *Les Bonnes Petites Tables du Guide Michelin*.

Three stars	Exceptional cuisine, worth a special journey
Two stars	Excellent cooking, worth a detour
One star	High-quality cooking, worth a stop
Bib gourmands	Good-quality, good-value cooking

The focus is on the quality of the ingredients, skill in preparation and in combining flavours, the personality of the chef conveyed through their cuisine, consistency of standards and value for money. Less emphasis is placed on décor and quality of service. Restaurants under consideration for stars are visited several times a year. France tops the charts as the country with the most stars but Tokyo leads the way as the city with the most three-starred restaurants.

ZAGAT

The New York-based dining guide Zagat, established in 1979 and now owned by Google, used to operate a thirty-point system for reviews based on food, décor and service and using ratings from restaurant-goers. It now scores restaurants on a sliding scale from one to five stars, taking into account online ratings and reviews, feedback from the public and diners on the ground to award points. The guide covers the USA, London, Toronto and Vancouver.

4.6–5.0 stars	Extraordinary to perfection
4.1–4.5 stars	Very good to excellent
3.1–4.0 stars	Good to very good
2.1–3.0 stars	Fair to good
1.0–2.0 stars	Poor to fair

The Danish Smiley System

Retail food enterprises in Denmark must comply with food regulations and are inspected, unannounced, between one and three times a year. In 2001 Smiley reports were introduced with smiley symbols awarded according to findings. In 2008 the 'Elite Smiley' came into being, awarded to those enterprises with four consecutive happy smiles in their inspection reports and no adverse comments in the last twelve months. Customers can view the pictorial ratings in supermarkets, restaurants, bakeries, butchers, grocery stores, hot dog stands, school canteens, care homes and hospital kitchens, and make informed choices about where to shop and eat. The smiles range from a very happy to a sour face, and inspection reports are published on findsmiley.dk

The elite smiley is awarded to those with the best inspection history.

No remarks.

Issued with an enjoining order or warning.

Issued with an injunction order or prohibition.

Administrative penalties, reported to the police, or approval withdrawn.

22   Table Etiquette

Modern formal dining in Western society is served *à la russe*. Courses are served in a fixed order from soup to dessert and coffee. This system is believed to have been introduced to France in the early nineteenth century by the Russian ambassador Prince Alexander Kurakin. It rapidly replaced the older system, *service à la française*, where all the dishes are put on the table at once. The new method imposed a hierarchy on the arrangement of cutlery/flatware, to help diners know in which order to use it. The general rule is to work from the outside in.

Setting for a four-course meal

From left to right

fish fork, dinner fork, salad fork, charger plate, dinner/steak knife, fish knife, soup spoon

The oyster fork, if used, is placed to the right of the soup spoon, angled so that the tines rest in the spoon bowl.

Above and slightly to left of forks

butter plate, butter knife placed diagonally, handle facing guest

Above and lightly right of knives

water glass, white wine glass, red wine glass, champagne glass

Above plate

dessert spoon (top), bowl facing left, dessert fork (below spoon), tines facing right (placed just before dessert is served, unless the main meal is only two courses)

CHARGER PLATE
This is a large plate that forms the base for the plates containing the first and fish courses; it is removed when the main course is served.

FIRST MENU
Service à la russe *saw the introduction of the menu, so that diners would know what they would be served as they could no longer see it spread out on the table.*

General rules

- Forks to the left, knives and spoons to the right.

- Knife blades face towards the plate.

- 15 inches/38 cm elbow room between each place setting.

- Cutlery/flatware aligns with the bottom of the plate, 1 inch/2.5 cm from the table edge.

- First item is 1 inch/2.5 cm from plate.

- No more than three utensils of the same type at any one time, with the exception of the oyster fork.

- Napkins are placed on the charger plate or to the left of the forks.

The US Government

The Constitution
The oldest written national constitution (1787) still in use, it defines the framework of the US federal government. The government is divided into three branches that are separate but equal to ensure no group or individual can gain too much control. Each branch can change/overturn acts and laws issued by the other branches in a system of checks and balances.

Legislative branch

Makes laws, confirms/rejects presidential appointments, and has the authority to declare war.

Congress (and agencies that provide help to Congress)
Confirms/rejects the President's appointments; it can remove the President from office in exceptional circumstances.

Senate
American citizens vote for two senators per state (one hundred in total); they serve for a term of six years, but there is no limit to the number of terms a senator can serve.

House of Representatives
American citizens vote for 435 representatives, divided among the fifty states proportionate to the state's population size. Representatives serve two-year terms with no limit to the number of terms.

Executive branch

Carries out and enforces laws.

President
The head of state, leader of the federal government and Commander-in-Chief of the US Armed forces. The President serves a four-year term, but for no more than two terms. The President can veto laws passed by Congress.

Vice President
Supports the President and assumes the presidency if the former is no longer able to serve. Can serve an unlimited number of four-year terms, although in practice no one has served more than two.

Cabinet
Cabinet members are nominated by the President (whom they advise) and are approved by the Senate. They include the Vice President and heads of fifteen executive departments. They are nominated by the President and must be approved by the Senate.

Other
Executive departments, independent agencies, boards and committees that help carry out the decisions made by government.

Judicial branch

Interprets the meaning of laws, applies them to individual cases, decides if they violate the Constitution.

Supreme court
Justices are appointed by the President and Senate, and can overturn unconstitutional laws. The Supreme Court comprises the Chief Justice and eight Associate Justices. Justices are appointed for life, but may retire or be removed in exceptional circumstances.

Other federal courts
Congress has the authority to create other federal courts. They try cases such as the constitutionality of a law involving public ministers, disputes between states, bankruptcy.

State courts
They try most criminal cases, probate, family law, tort, etc.

All the Presidents' Men

Should a president die, resign, fail to qualify, be removed or unable to discharge the powers and duties of office, the Constitution of the United States and Presidential Succession Act of 1947 have got it covered. Next in line is the Vice President and should something befall him or her the baton passes to the Speaker of the House of Representatives. Stepping into the breach next is the President Pro Tempore of the Senate (the most senior member of the majority party), in whose potentially vacant footsteps would come the Cabinet members, with their eligibility based on the date their offices were established.

The 25th Amendment of the Constitution, ratified in 1967, allows the Vice President to step into the presidential chair during illness or a temporary inability to fulfil duties. In 1985 Ronald Reagan put George H. W. Bush in charge when he underwent surgery.

Potential line of succession:

Vice President
Speaker of the House of Representatives
President Pro Tempore of the Senate
Secretary of State
Secretary of the Treasury
Secretary of Defense
Attorney General
Secretary of the Interior
Secretary of Agriculture
Secretary of Commerce
Secretary of Labor
Secretary of Health and Human Services
Secretary of Housing and Urban Development
Secretary of Transportation
Secretary of Energy
Secretary of Education
Secretary of Veteran Affairs
Secretary of Homeland Security

DESIGNATED SURVIVOR
In the event of a State of the Union address or a presidential inauguration at which the president and all successors are due to be present, a 'designated survivor' stays behind in a secure location.

Higher-Archy

The best seats in the house at the Amphitheatrum Flavian, otherwise known as the Colosseum, in Ancient Rome, were reserved for the imperial family, naturally. Entrance was free, although spectators needed some form of ticket (*tessera*), but egalitarianism came to a shuddering halt right there as seating depended on wealth, gender, religious affiliation and social status. The seating itself was made up of tiers that reflected the stratified nature of Roman society. Visitors would have been guided to the appropriate archway (out of a total of eighty), and then entered via different internal passageways and staircases.

Cubiculum

Imperial boxes at the north and south end were reserved for the emperor and his family, the social elite and Vestal Virgins (the only female priests of Rome). It is likely that sons of the emperor and other male relatives, along with esteemed guests, also sat here.

Podium

Meaning place of honour, it was on the same level as the cubiculum, and was reserved for the senators in their white togas edged with purple/crimson stripes and the most important priests. Some would bring their own chairs.

Maenianum primum

The next level down was for non-senatorial nobility and knights (*equites*).

Maenianum secundum

Reserved for the general body of Roman citizens in their off-white togas. The immum, or lower part, was for the wealthy, and the summum, or upper part, for the poor, including slaves in their belted woollen tunics.

Maenianum secundum in ligneis

This was a gallery of steep wooden seats around the top of the auditorium that was set up later in the reign of Emperor Domitian, where women from all classes sat.

PERSONA NON GRATA
Banned from the amphitheatre were former gladiators, gravediggers and actors.

Gladiatorial Combat

In the early days of the Roman Empire, slaves, prisoners of war and criminals were forced to train in the gladiator schools to fight in the arena in front of the bloodthirsty crowds. Later in the empire's history, free men sometimes also enrolled, attracted by the prospect of glory and money if successful – gladiators could keep any prizes or gifts received during the games. A loose hierarchy evolved among them, based on experience and the sheer ability to stay alive, and to an extent upon the type of fighting in which they specialised.

Rudiarius

Elite gladiators who had fought so bravely and well that they had obtained their freedom. They could retire completely or work in some capacity, often as a bodyguard or training other gladiators, or could choose to carry on in the arena, soaking up the adulation of the mob. A *rudiarius* could never become a Roman citizen, although his children could.

Primus palus

A top-ranking gladiator. *Primus palus* translates as first pole. The gladiators trained by slashing at poles (*pali*) fixed in the ground.

Secundus palus

A second-ranking gladiator, 'second pole'; followed by 'third pole', 'fourth pole', and so on.

Veteranus

A gladiator (a 'swordsman' from *gladius*, sword) who had survived his first fight.

Tiro

A trained novice gladiator deemed ready for his first fight.

Novicius

A trainee gladiator.

GLADIATORS GOT TALENT

Gladiators were trained to fight in one of numerous different ways. Some combat specialisms were regarded as more elite than others, e.g. the sagittarius, *a skilled bowman on horseback, who was popular with the crowd, unlike the hapless* retiarius, *who fought with a net requiring evasive tactics that the crowd deemed unmanly. And some were more heavily armed (e.g.* hoplomachus *with sword, dagger, lance) than others (e.g.* lacquerarius, *with one weapon and a lasso). Differing specialisms were paired specifically to produce an entertaining combat.*

The Roman Senate

The Roman Republic was an ancient state that existed for nearly five hundred years, from 509 BC until the establishment of the Roman Empire in 27 BC. Its complex form of government, with a constitution of sorts, laws and elected officials, bore a marked resemblance to modern democracies, although there were disparities based on social class, wealth and gender (women could neither vote nor hold office). The Republic was run by a Senate headed by two Consuls, all of whom were patricians – members of a noble family or class. However, there was considerable input from the Assembly, which comprised the plebeians, or commoners – the (male) citizens of Rome.

Consuls

The Assembly elected the two consuls from the Senate by majority vote. Consuls served a one-year term; their duties were to oversee the work of other government officials, command the army, act as judges, and select a new Senate member in the event of a senator's death. In times of crisis requiring prompt action, the consuls could appoint a 'dictator', who was in command until the crisis was resolved. Importantly, the Consuls had to agree on decisions and each had the power to veto the other – this overcame the risk of one consul taking total control.

Proconsuls

A proconsul was a governor appointed by the Senate to rule provinces conquered by Rome, many of which were relatively far-flung. The proconsuls had much the same authority as the consuls.

The Senate

The three hundred members of the Senate (derived from the Latin senex, meaning 'old man') were sandwiched between the Consuls above them and the Assembly below, and advised both. They had the power to approve or disapprove laws proposed by the Assembly and make decisions on finance and foreign policy. Once elected, a senator was in post for life.

Specialist Senate posts included:

Praetors
Magistrates ranked immediately below the consuls, to whom they acted as deputy when necessary. They were also in

charge of the judiciary and were responsible for staging the public games that were a feature of life in Ancient Rome.

Censor
Official responsible for overseeing the census. He also had the power to promote or demote individuals with regard to social class.

Aediles
Officials responsible for the maintenance of public buildings and roads and the regulation of festivals.

Quaestors
Officials in charge of public revenue and expenditure.

The Assembly

In addition to electing the two consuls, the Assembly – or Plebeian Council – elected government officials (including judges), voted on laws proposed by government officials (and vetoed them, if required, through representatives known as tribunes), and declared war or peace, as appropriate.

PS & QS

As the Roman Republic became established, plebeians were able to rise to higher ranks of office. For example, in 409 BC the first plebeian Quaestor – the lowest-ranking magistrate – was appointed; in 356 BC the first plebeian dictator was appointed, later taking the position of Censor; while 337 BC saw the elevation of a plebeian to the post of Praetor.

The Cosa Nostra

With its origins in medieval Sicily, the organised crime of the Mafia began to take a foothold in the United States in the late nineteenth century. By the early 1930s, bolstered by the large number of Italian immigrants, the American Mafia had become tremendously powerful, ousting rival gangs and seizing control of their illegal activities. They adopted the name that would come to strike a chill in the heart of anyone not connected with 'the family' – the 'Cosa Nostra', or 'Our Affair', 'Our Thing'.

Commission
Made up of the heads of the most powerful Mafia 'families' or factions. Only the Commission can challenge the authority of a Boss.

Boss/Don
Head of the family, feared and very wealthy thanks to the 'tribute' or cut he receives from the entire family's earnings. He makes all the important decisions.

Consigliere A trusted friend and confidant who acts as a counsellor to the Boss and mediator in disputes.

Underboss
The powerful number two – often a direct blood family member – he is groomed to take over from the Boss. He runs the family's day-to-day operations and receives a percentage earnings cut from the Boss.

Caporegime/Capo
He carries out the orders of the Boss and Underboss, and is in charge of a crew of ten to twenty soldiers. He also acts as a buffer, distancing the Boss from what otherwise might be a too-direct association with the family's activities.

Soldato/Soldier
One of the 'boots on the ground' who carries out the family's dirty work – intimidation, extortion, murder . . . A 'made man' who must be of Italian descent and take an oath of *omertà* – silence and non-cooperation with the authorities.

Associate
Not yet an official member of the Mafia, he runs errands and carries out small jobs for those above. An Associate aspires to prove his worth and become a 'made man'.

29　The Triads

A secret society that originated in China, today the triads are crime gangs that still work to strict rules with the swearing of an oath and a Mafia-like tradition of mutual assistance. They are active on an international scale, including in major cities in the UK, North America, Australia and New Zealand. The triads use numeric codes based on Chinese numerology to differentiate between the ranks of their members and have a system of secret signs and tattoos through which they can communicate clandestinely.

Shan Chu 489
Mountain/Dragon Master
Group leader

Fu Shan Chu 438
Deputy Mountain
Master
Deputy leader

Heung Chu 438
Incense Master
Performs initiation
and promotion
ceremonies and
rituals

Sin Fung 438
Vanguard
Recruits members,
organises
and assists at
ceremonies

Pak Tsz Sin 415
White Paper Fan
Administrative officer. Advises on business and finance

Hung Kwan 426
Red Pole
Commands units of fifty men. Oversees offensive and
defensive operations. Red Poles have a background
in the military

Cho Hai 432
Straw Sandal or Glass Slipper
Organises meetings and gang fights. Liaises between units

Chai 49
Ordinary gang member
New recruits and triad foot soldiers

Blue Lanterns
Uninitiated members
(No code)

The Knights Templar

Members of a religious military order established to protect Christian Crusaders, the Knights Templar in their distinctive white surcoat with a red cross have become associated with legend and mystery. The Crusades, mounted to halt Muslim expansion into the Holy Land, began in 1095 and continued until the fall of the last Crusader stronghold in 1291, and thereafter, with rather less zeal, until the sixteenth-century Protestant Reformation heralded the decline of papal authority. However, the Order itself was annihilated in 1307, falsely accused of blasphemy by King Philip IV of France, who was in need of the Order's vast wealth. Many of its members were put through seven years of inquisition, followed by public execution.

Grand Master

In overall charge of the Order worldwide. It was an elected office, held for life – that of the last Master, Jacques de Molay, came to a gruesome end when he was burnt at the stake, declaring: 'God will avenge our deaths.'

Master and Commander

A local commander, in control of a small Templar stronghold known as a commandery.

Seneschal	The Master's right-hand man, who in peacetime administered the Order's lands and in wartime masterminded the practical stuff – moving men and their pack trains, and procuring food.
Turcopolier	In command of the light cavalry and the Sergeant brothers.
Marshal	In charge of arms and horses.
Under-Marshal	In charge of the horses' tack.
Standard Bearer	In charge of the squires. Despite his name, he marched in front of the banner, rather than 'bearing' it himself.
Knight	Armour-clad and skilled in warfare, the knights were the backbone of the battlefield.
Sergeant	A light cavalry officer, and support for the noble knights, usually of a lower social class. Sergeants wore a black or brown mantle over their black tunic, often with a red cross like the Knights.
Treasurer	In charge of the books, a responsible position as the Knights Templar were a very wealthy order.
Draper	In charge of clothing and bed linen.
Squires	Assistants to the knights.
Lay servants	Their duties varied widely, depending on whose servant they were.
Chaplains (a separate class from the knights)	They were responsible for conducting religious services, administering the sacraments, and addressing the spiritual needs of the Templars.

UNLUCKY FOR SOME

Among the legends that have grown up around the Templars over the centuries are their associations with freemasonry, the Holy Grail and with Scotland – in particular with Rosslyn Chapel near Edinburgh. They have also been credited as the source of the unlucky day Friday 13th – many were arrested in the Templar purge on Friday 13th, 1307. And not forgetting the legend of the lost Templar treasure that is still waiting to be found ... somewhere.

The British Army

The system of officer ranks is the backbone of an army's hierarchy. It makes clear the role and responsibility of a soldier. The ranking systems are multitudinous, varying across conflicts and eras. Here is the officer ranking structure in today's British Army, as detailed on its website: www.army.mod.uk.

General
(aka 4 star)

Holds the most senior positions, e.g. Chief of Defence Staff, Deputy Supreme Allied Commander Europe, Commander in Chief Land Forces.

Lieutenant General
(aka 3 star)

Commands formations of corps size and other commands in the UK and overseas. Holds very senior staff appointments in the Ministry of Defence.

Major General
(aka 2 star)

Commands formations of division size. Holds senior staff appointments in the Ministry of Defence and other headquarters.

Brigadier
(aka 1 star)

A field officer rank. Commands a brigade or can be a director of operational capability groups, such as a director of staff.

Colonel

Does not normally command in the field, but serves as a staff officer between field commands at battalion/brigade level. Also principal operational advisor to senior officers.

Lieutenant Colonel

Responsible for the overall operational effectiveness, welfare and discipline of a unit of up to 650 soldiers, comprising four or five sub-units.

Major	Usually after eight to ten years' service, commands a sub-unit of up to 120 officers and soldiers.
Captain	Typically the second-in-command of a sub-unit of up to 120 soldiers. Plays a key role in planning and decision-making processes.
Lieutenant	A post usually held for up to three years, in command of a platoon or troop of around thirty soldiers.
Second Lieutenant	The first commissioned rank, normally held for up to two years.
Officer Cadet	The rank held during initial officer training at the Royal Military Academy Sandhurst.

SUBALTERN

From the Latin alternus *(alternate), a subaltern is technically any commissioned officer below the rank of captain, but it often refers to a second lieutenant.*

PRIVATE PRIVATES

The Atholl Highlanders, employed privately by the Scottish Duke of Atholl, is Europe's only legal private regiment and not part of the British Army. It was originally formed in 1777 to fight with the British Army in the American Revolutionary War, but now performs ceremonial duties.

The Roman Army

Although it changed over the centuries, for many people the archetypal Roman army of popular imagination is that of the post-Marian Reforms of 107 BC (military reforms initiated by general and statesman Gaius Marius), structured largely as follows (the exact numbers of troops per unit varies slightly according to source). It was a professional standing army of volunteers comprising around thirty legions.

Each legion had auxiliary units such as archers or cavalry attached to it. Soldiers performing special duties included a *cornicen* who would sound a large circular trumpet to signal orders, and an a*quilifer*, who carried the legion's standard, representing its honour.

Legio
(Legion)

Comprised ten cohorts (nine + the double-strength First Cohort), totalling around 5,500 men. Commanded by a *Legatus Legionis*, assisted by various officers including several tribunes and a *Praefectus castrorum* (camp prefect), a veteran soldier who was third in command of the legion (after the *legatus* and *tribunus*).

Cohors Prima
(First Cohort)

Comprised five double-size *centuriae*, therefore totalling eight hundred men, excluding officers. They included elite troops and specialists in some form of trade (blacksmiths, construction, etc.).

Cohortes I – IX
(cohorts 1–9)

Each comprised six *centuriae*, therefore totalling 480 men, excluding officers.

Centuria
(century)

Comprised ten *conturbenia*, therefore totalling eighty men, excluding officers. Commanded by a centurion, assisted by several officers, including the *optio*, second in command. The First Cohort's centurion was the *primus pilus* (first spear), the highest-ranking centurion in the legion.

Conturbenium

The smallest unit, a group of eight soldiers who shared a tent. Commanded by a *decanus*.

The Roman Catholic Church

Derived from the Greek word *katholikos*, meaning 'universal', the Catholic Church dates its foundation to the Christian community established by Jesus. The Church was established in Rome by the apostle Peter, bynamed 'The Rock' as he would be the foundation upon which the Church was built. Jesus nominated Peter as the first pope, and all subsequent popes – 265 to date – are considered Peter's successors. As the Church grew, it became necessary to appoint a clergy to act in persona Christi Capitis (in the person of Christ, the Head [of the Church]). The clergy – currently all-male – is ordained through the Sacrament of Holy Orders and divided into the Episcopate, the Priesthood and the Deaconate.

THE EPISCOPATE

POPE

The Bishop of Rome, head of the Roman Catholic Church, and the only bishop who can speak on behalf of the entire Church. The Pope's cathedral church is St Peter's Basilica in the heart of the Vatican City, the 44-hectare (109-acre) independent papal state in Rome.

CARDINAL

Cardinals are nominated by the pope and form the Sacred College, responsible since 1059 for electing succeeding popes – prior to that, popes were elected by the clergy and laity of Rome. Since 1378, when Urban VI, a non-cardinal, was elected, all popes have been elected from within the Sacred College. There are currently 223 cardinals worldwide, of which only 117 are electors, the remainder being over the age of eighty and therefore no longer eligible to vote.

ARCHBISHOP

The chief bishop (see below) of a diocese considered important because of its size and/or historical significance. In the Church of England, established in 1534, the Archbishop of Canterbury is the equivalent of the Pope in his role as senior bishop and principal leader of the Anglican Church (Canterbury has been the seat of Christianity in Britain since 597 AD).

BISHOP

A successor of the apostles and responsible for a diocese, made up of local parishes. Only bishops may confer the Sacrament of Holy Orders and consecrate Chrism (sacramental oil).

THE PRIESTHOOD

DIOCESAN PRIEST

A co-worker of a bishop and usually ordained by the bishop in whose diocese he will serve. A diocesan priest may be conferred with the title 'Monsignor', establishing the priest as a member of the papal household.

VICAR GENERAL

An assistant to the bishop, assisting in the governance of a diocese.

ARCHPRIEST OR VICAR FORANE

A priest in charge of a *vicariate forane* (a group of parishes within a diocese), who assists the priests of those parishes.

PARISH PRIEST OR PASTOR

Responsible for the pastoral care of the laity in a parish within the diocese.

PAROCHIAL VICAR

An assistant to a parish priest.

THE DEACONATE

DEACON

The lowest rank of ordained minister who assists in preaching the Gospel, but, unlike those in the episcopate and priesthood, has no special charisma (divinely conferred power). A 'transitional' deacon is one who intends to become a priest, while a 'permanent' deacon will remain a deacon.

PAPAL CONCLAVE

Cardinals electing a new pope gather in the Sistine Chapel in the Apostolic Palace, the Pope's official residence, where they vote for their favoured candidate. A candidate requires two-thirds of the vote to ascend, and the process doesn't always go smoothly – in 1378, for example, failure to agree led to the Western Schism, a split within the Catholic Church that lasted until 1417.

The Church of England

The Protestant Church of England was established when King Henry VIII broke with the Roman Catholic Church in order to divorce his wife, Catherine of Aragon (who had failed to produce a male heir to the throne), and marry Anne Boleyn (who also failed to produce a male heir, but that's another story ...). In 1534 Henry passed the Act of Supremacy, which recognised him as the 'only supreme head of the Church of England called *Anglicana Ecclesia*'. His daughter Queen Elizabeth I declared herself Supreme Governor of the Church of England, a title passed down through the royal line of succession and today held by Queen Elizabeth II. The Church is divided into areas of ever-decreasing size, as follows:

Province
There are two provinces, south and north. The south is led by the Archbishop of Canterbury and the north by the Archbishop of York.

Diocese or See
A large area under the authority of a bishop. The word 'see' is derived from the Latin *sedes*, meaning 'seat'.

Cathedral
A cathedral contains the bishop's seat or throne, and is run by the dean and chapter. The chapter typically includes a chancellor, precentor (leads the congregation in singing), pastor, archdeacon, treasurer, canons (clergy members who are part of the chapter) and a clerk. The term 'chapter' is derived from the sixth-century Rule of St Benedict, which included a directive that monks should gather daily for the reading of a chapter of the Bible.

Archdeaconry
A smaller area within a diocese, under the authority of an archdeacon.

Deanery
A group of parishes within a diocese, under the care of a rural dean (as distinct from a cathedral dean).

Parish
The smallest division, under a vicar or, historically, a rector, dating from an age where tithes were payable to the incumbent.

Ecclesiastical Courts

Prior to the late 1850s, when national courts were established, many legal matters were administered through a hierarchy of ecclesiastical courts, similar to the secular courts of today, but with more interesting – and even peculiar – names.

Royal Peculiar
(with courts)

A 'peculiar' is a church that is outside the jurisdiction of the diocese in which it is located, and most are 'royal' – they owe their allegiance directly to the sovereign. Westminster Abbey (where all British monarchs have been crowned since 1066) is an example of a Royal Peculiar.

Prerogative Court

The provincial court of the Archbishops of Canterbury and York – effectively the Supreme Court of the Church.

Consistory Court

The court of a bishop. Consistory courts were established shortly after the Norman Conquest in 1066 and dealt with cases of defamation, probate and matrimony as well as Church-related matters.

Archdeaconry Court

The court of an archdeacon. Until minor criminal jurisdiction passed to Justices of the Peace in the eighteenth century, it was the responsibility of the archdeaconry court.

Decanal Court

The court of a dean. The word 'decanal' is derived from the Latin *decanus*, meaning 'chief of a group of ten' (in this case, the chapter).

Peculiar Court

Again, a non-royal 'peculiar' is outside the jurisdiction of the diocese in which it is located, but in this case it is related, for example, to the chapel of a school, university or the Inns of Court in London.

FIRST AMONG EQUALS

The Archbishops of Canterbury and York originally had equal status, but in 1071 the Pope declared that Canterbury should take precedence. This was eventually formalised by an Act of Parliament in the reign of Henry VIII, and today the Archbishop of Canterbury is recognised as primus inter pares – 'first among equals'.

35 The Church of Jesus Christ of Latter-Day Saints

The Church (aka LDS) was founded in 1830 with the publication of the Book of Mormon, which adherents believe is an English translation of a sacred Hebrew text relating the story of Israelite peoples who lived in America in ancient times. The existence of the text, said to have been lost for 1,500 years, was revealed by the Angel Moroni to Joseph Smith, who organised the LDS with a small group of believers. After Smith was murdered by an anti-Mormon mob, his successor, Brigham Young, led an exodus to Utah and established the Mormon settlement of Salt Lake City.

The Church, whose members are known as Mormons, is overseen by fifteen apostles, considered the 'special witnesses' of Jesus Christ. There are also local congregations with their own hierarchy.

CHURCH LEADERS

FIRST PRESIDENCY

The Church's highest governing body. It consists of the president, the most senior apostle, considered God's spokesman on Earth, and two counsellors chosen by the president. The First Presidency of the Early Church comprised the apostles Peter, James and John, selected by Christ.

QUORUM OF THE TWELVE

These apostles are the second-highest governing body. Traditionally, the original apostles number twelve in total, but the LDS interpretation of the New Testament has isolated the First Presidency, making the total fifteen.

SEVENTIES

The Quorum of the Twelve is assisted by a third level of leaders called 'seventies', who serve in various locations worldwide. They are so named because each group has up to seventy members, a reference to the seventy disciples of Christ mentioned in the Gospel of Luke. The Seventies are further divided into the Seven Presidents, the First Quorum and the Second Quorum.

LOCAL CONGREGATIONS

STAKE PRESIDENT

Local congregations are made up of administrative parishes called wards. A group of wards forms a stake, headed by the stake president, an unsalaried position. A stake president serves for about nine years.

BISHOP

The leader of a ward, a bishop serves for about five years. This post is also unsalaried.

MEMBERS

The members of the Church themselves assist the local leaders in the administration of the wards.

THE STAKE

The term 'stake' derives from the Old Testament, referring to the stakes that supported the tabernacle, or tent – effectively a church, albeit a mobile one, and symbolically 'the Church'.

THE ANGEL MORONI

Most Mormon temples display a statue of the Angel Moroni. They are all replicas of one of six versions of the statue; the first official Moroni, sculpted for the Salt Lake Temple, was covered in 22-carat gold leaf. Moronis located on top of a temple usually face east, and all hold a trumpet in the right hand, symbolising spreading the gospel and the Second Coming of Jesus Christ.

Shinto

Derived from the Chinese *shéndào*, meaning 'the way of the gods', Shinto is a Japanese religion combining worship of ancestors and nature spirits with a belief in sacred power (*kami*) in all things, animate and inanimate. Visiting shrines is an important aspect of Shinto, and since 1946, when the Emperor, also the high priest of Shinto, lost his divine status in Japan's Allied occupation following World War II, the shrine priesthood (*shinshoku*), traditionally hereditary, has become a profession requiring an advanced level of study. The hierarchy of qualifications, from lowest to highest, is:

Chokkai (uprightness)   The beginners' rank – entry level.

Gonseikai   Gonseikai priests are qualified to serve at village or township shrines. Candidates for this rank must display knowledge of Shinto shrines and ritual, including old customs, as well as Japanese history, ethics, literature, the *Kojiki* (Record of Ancient Matters) and invocational prayers (*norito*).

Seikai
(righteousness)   The qualification required to serve as head priest at prefecture-level shrines or as a lower-ranked priest (*Negi*) at shrines nationwide. To achieve this rank, candidates must expand the knowledge required for the rank of Gonseikai to include shrine etiquette, philosophy, psychology, world religions, and the *Nihon shoki* ('The Chronicles of Japan').

Meikai (brightness)

The qualification required to serve as head priest (*Guji*) or assistant priest (*Gonguji*) at shrines nationwide. Candidates must expand the knowledge required for the rank of Seikai to include the regulations contained in the *Engi Shiki* ('Institutes of the Engi Period'), Shinto documents, ancient rules and traditions, as well as history of religion (including Buddhism and Christianity) and world history. They must also perform a ritual.

Jokai (purity)

The highest rank, awarded to those who have carried out many years' study of Shinto practice. It is achieved through recommendation rather than passing a test of knowledge.

IMPERIAL DIVINITY

The spiritual status of the emperor of Japan as descendant of the sun goddess Amaterasu became official doctrine around the eighth century AD, and even in modern-day Japan the Grand Shrine and sub-shrines of Ise, devoted to Amaterasu, play a key role in Shintoism. The high priest and priestess of the Grand Shrine of Ise are usually members or descendants of the imperial family.

STATE SHINTO

State Shinto, with the emperor and the ceremonies of the imperial household at its heart, was established in 1868 in the Meiji era. It was the official state religion until 1946 when an imperial rescript was issued in which Emperor Hirohito declared that he was not a living god.

In Japanese sumo, wrestlers, or *rikishi*, use their weight, bulk and strength to force their opponent out of a 4.6m/15ft diameter ring, or to put any part of their body on the ground other than the soles of their feet. Around 550 *rikishi* of various ranks compete in six divisions at any given time. The wrestlers move up and down the rankings depending on their performance in preceding tournaments, except for the highly respected *yokozuna* at the very top of the hierarchy. *Rikishi* are ranked numerically in descending order and are divided into east (most prestigious) and west groups, so the top rank in, say, s*andanme* is s*andanme* 1 east, and the second rank *sandanme* 1 west, followed by the third rank *sandanme* 2 east, and so on.

THE DIVISIONS

The number of wrestlers competing in each division is limited. Each wrestler belongs to a stable (*heya*) of three to twenty *rikishi* of different ranks. The lower ranking wrestlers train and live at the stable full-time.

MAKUUCHI
The top division
Forty-two *rikishi*

JŪRYŌ
Twenty-eight *rikishi*

MAKUSHITA
One hundred and twenty *rikishi*

SANDANME
Around two hundred *rikishi*

JONIDAN
Around two hundred and fifty *rikishi*

JONOKUCHI
Around eighty *rikishi*

MAKUUCHI RANKS

YOKOZUNA (grand champion)
Excelling in skill, strength and, importantly, also in dignity and grace, only just over seventy *rikishi* have achieved this rank to date since 1630, and there have been periods when no wrestlers at all have qualified to compete at this level. Unlike the rest of the ranks, *yokozuna* cannot be demoted

but are expected to retire when they can no longer perform at their peak, even during a tournament (*honbasho*).

ŌZEKI

A wrestler is considered for promotion (discretionary) to *ōzeki* if he wins thirty-three bouts over three consecutive tournaments. Perks include acting as dewsweeper or swordbearer for a *yokozuna*'s ring-entering ceremony and having junior wrestlers as personal attendants. The *banzuke* (official list of the rankings) requires there to be a minimum of two *ōzeki* at any one time, one east and one west.

SEKIWAKE

A wrestler needs a good record of wins in previous tournaments to be promoted to *sekiwake* and for there to be space available at that rank. There should be a minimum of two *sekiwake* at any one time (east and west).

KOMUSUBI

To achieve this rank, *rikishi* must have achieved more wins than defeats in a tournament. There should be a minimum of two *komusubi* at any one time (east and west).

MAEGASHIRA

The remaining *rikishi* in the Makuuchi division, usually around thirty-two in total (sixteen east, sixteen west) depending on their performance at their previous tournament.

SEKITORI

Wrestlers in the top two divisions (makuuchi and jūryō), are also known as sekitori. They wear their hair in an ōichō (topknot fanned out into the shape of a ginkgo leaf, styled by specialist hairdressers), wear colourful mawashi (belts) and can take part in ring-entering ceremonies. They are assigned lower-ranked wrestlers as personal attendants who are expected to wash their underwear, clean their rooms, serve their meals, run errands, etc. Sekitori are also allowed to get married and live away from the stable.

38

Judo

Dr Jigorō Kanō of Japan, founder of modern judo, came up with the coloured belt system to indicate the progress of students or *judoka*, and the first black belts were awarded in the 1880s. This system became the basis for modern martial arts. *Judoka* usually start with a white belt and the colours gradually become darker as skill and knowledge increase. Colours and standards can vary quite widely according to country but in western judo usually follow the order below, with six student grades or *kyu*, leading up to the coveted black belt when a *judoka* becomes a *dan* or advanced grade holder. The belt colours of the twelve advanced *dan* levels are more consistent across clubs and countries.

Judo places great emphasis on self-discipline and respect for others, and lower ranks are expected to show respect to *judoka* of more senior rank. Skill in practice and contest along with technical knowledge are required to advance to 5th *dan*, after which advancement for the *yudansha* ('person who has *dan*') is based on service to the sport.

ENTRY LEVEL	6th kyu	white belt
	5th kyu	yellow belt
	4th kyu	orange
	3rd kyu	green
	2nd kyu	blue
	1st kyu	brown
ADVANCED	1st to 5th dan	black
	6th to 8th dan	red-and-white
	9th to 11th dan	red
	12th dan	wider version of the white belt

Karate

Gichin Funakoshi, a friend of judo founder Dr Kanō, adopted judo's belt system and other fundamental characteristics for karate. Known as the grandfather of Japanese karate, he founded Shotokan, one of the most popular styles of karate today. Different styles of karate have different belt colours but generally begin with a white belt. A black belt is issued when a *karateka* (student of karate) has achieved a level of training and expertise that means they can then teach. The student ranking system includes ten *kyus* – *kyu* means grades away from the black belt or *dan*.

Shokotan karate kyu belts (lowest to highest)

10th	Jik-kyu	white
9th	Kyo-kyu	orange
8th	Hachi-kyu	red
7th	Schichi-kyu	yellow
6th	Rok-kyu	green
5th	Go-kyu	purple
4th	Yon-kyu	purple/white
3rd	San-kyu	second purple
2nd	Ni-kyu	first brown
1st	Ik-kyu	second brown, third brown/white, or black

There are ten levels of black belt or *dan*, and each level takes longer than the last to achieve. The first few *dan* grades are awarded on physical ability but higher levels are based on teaching experience, leadership, tenure and service to the organisation. Vladimir Putin was awarded the 8th *dan* in 2012, the first Russian to achieve this.

Dan level (highest to lowest, all black belt)

10th	Jyu-dan
9th	Ky-dan
8th	Hachi-dan
7th	Schichi-dan
6th	Roku-dan
5th	Go-dan
4th	Yon-dan
3rd	San-dan
2nd	Ni-dan
1st	Sho-dan

BELT UP

The obi, *or belt, is worn around the waist as an indicator of the level of experience and training, and for practical purposes, keeping the jacket or* uwagi *closed and providing some protection for the vital organs. Traditionally gis (karate uniforms) were white but students today may wear a coloured uniform (e.g. red, blue).*

The Jedi Order

The Jedi (founded c. 25,000 BBY – before the Battle of Yavin) are adherents of the Force, a network of energy that connects all living things in the galaxy. They are members of an ancient monastic organisation that aims to promote peace and provide support to the weak, while continuing study of the Force.

Jedi initiate or youngling

A child who is 'Force-sensitive'. Younglings are frequently sent away from the parental home to the Jedi Academy at a young age (varies according to species, four or five years for humans). There they are instructed by Jedi Masters, learning simple basic control over the Force and self-defence techniques.

Padawan

Jedi knights or masters choose a youngling to become their pupil. Younglings not chosen for special instruction may enter the Jedi Service Corps to specialise in, say, agriculture or exploration. Before being allowed to take the initiate Trials to Knighthood, padawans must construct their own lightsaber.

Knight

A padawan who has successfully completed the Trials, including the Trial of Flesh, the Trial of Courage, the Trial of Skill, the Trial of Spirit and the Trial of Insight.

Master

A Jedi Knight who has performed a deed deemed extraordinary or exceptional in some way, or who has trained a padawan to be eligible for promotion to the rank of knight.

Grand Master

The head of the order and leader of the Jedi governing body, the High Council. A very experienced Jedi Master, particularly noted for their wisdom, and often the most senior Jedi Master. They guide the Order and oversee its activities.

TO THE CAVES OF ILUM, MUST YOU GO
As part of the Jedi tradition, initiates taking part in the ritual known as The Gathering travel to the Crystal Caves of Ilum to find a kyber crystal that is in tune with their individual awareness of the Force. The kyber crystal is a crucial component, being the source of the lightsaber's power.

Starfleet

Starfleet's deep-space exploration really took off with the development of the first warp five speed craft (*Enterprise* NX-01) in the 2150s, and continued after the founding of the United Federation of Planets in 2161. As a result, Starfleet's officers frequently assume the role of ambassador, often representing the first contact a civilisation has with the Federation. The organisation also takes on diplomatic (escorting dignitaries) and humanitarian (no matter what species) functions, as well as playing a defensive role. Starfleet's officer ranks are based on the naval ranks used on Earth. Cadets normally spend four years at Starfleet Academy in San Francisco, Earth, before graduating in one of three divisions: command (starships, starbases, Starfleet HQ), operations (operational departments of a starship, e.g. engineering) and science (research and medical). Promotion is strictly on the basis of merit.

At least one officer of distinction in Starfleet's long history is listed for each of the senior ranks given overleaf, although a number of them went on to reach a higher rank than the one listed. All those listed served in the twenty-third or twenty-fourth centuries:

Flag officers	**Commander-in-Chief** – top ranking Fleet Admiral, commands the entire Starfleet – C. in C. Bill
	Fleet Admiral – Harry Morrow
	Admiral – Charlie Whatley
	Vice Admiral – Kathryn Janeway
	Rear Admiral – Erik Pressman
	Commodore – Robert Wesley, USS *Lexington*
Officers	**Fleet Captain** – Christopher Pike
	Captain – Jean-Luc Picard ; James Tiberius Kirk of the USS *Enterprise* NCC-1701
	Commander – William T. Riker
	Lieutenant commander (usually a departmental head) – Montgomery Scott; Geordi La Forge (engineering); Leonard McCoy (medicine); Spock (science)
	Lieutenant – Nyota Uhura (communications); Hikaru Sulu (navigation)
	Lieutenant Junior Grade – Dr Julian Bashir; Worf (Klingon)
	Ensign – Pavel Chekov; Harry Kim
Junior officers and crewmen	**Master chief petty officer**
	Senior chief petty officer
	Chief petty officer
	Petty officer first class
	Petty officer second class
	Crewman first class
	Crewman second class
	Crewman third class

The Zodiacal Constellations

Constellations are the human imposition of patterns on the heavens; the stars in a constellation are rarely grouped together physically, and many are light years apart. There are eighty-eight constellations altogether, of which the oldest established are the twelve zodiac constellations visible to everybody on Earth the whole year round. They occupy a narrow but busy band of sky, the ecliptic, which is the apparent path of the Sun as it rolls round the year, and the orbital plane of the Moon and the visible planets (Mercury, Venus, Mars, Jupiter, Saturn). The constellations provide a useful coordinate system to locate the Sun and the planets as they appear to pass in front of them.

The modern order of the astronomical zodiac was established by the Hellenic scholar Ptolemy (AD 90–168) some 2,000 years ago, starting with Aries, which marked the position of the Sun at the spring equinox in the northern hemisphere. The chart shows the astronomical zodiac constellations in order of size. In order of sequence, both astrologically and astronomically, the zodiac starts with Aries and ends with Pisces, as listed.

CELESTIAL BESTIARY
These twelve constellations are known as the zodiac, from the Greek word zoidion, *meaning little animal, as most of them are imagined as real or mythical beasts.*

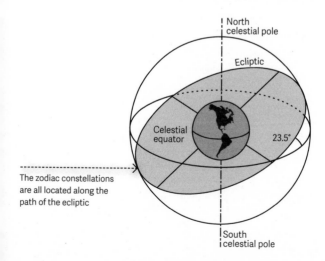

The zodiac constellations are all located along the path of the ecliptic

Zodiacal constellation sequence

Aries	Libra
Taurus	Scorpio
Gemini	Sagittarius
Cancer	Capricorn
Leo	Aquarius
Virgo	Pisces

By size

Virgo   3.1 per cent of sky
Brightest star: Spica

Aquarius   2.4 per cent of sky
Brightest star: Sadalsuud

Leo   2.3 per cent of sky
Brightest star: Regulus

Pisces   2.2 per cent of sky
Brightest star: Alpherg or Kullut Nunu

Sagittarius   2.1 per cent of sky
Brightest star: Kaus Australis

Taurus   1.9 per cent of sky
Brightest star: Aldebaran

Libra   1.3 per cent of sky
Brightest star: Zubeneschamali

Gemini   1.2 per cent of sky
Brightest star: Pollux

Cancer   1.2 per cent of sky
Brightest star: Altarf

Scorpio   1.2 per cent of sky
Brightest star: Antares

Aries   1.1 per cent of sky
Brightest star: Hamal

Capricorn   1.0 per cent of sky
Brightest star: Deneb Algedi

NASA Astronauts

From the Greek term meaning 'space sailor', astronauts are men and women who boldly go into space, in this case for America's National Aeronautics and Space Administration. Their missions have varied over the years, but with the ending of the space shuttle in 2011 and until a mission to Mars becomes more of a reality, astronauts currently aspire to join the International Space Station (ISS) orbiting the Earth. It is an egalitarian profession – there is no room for egos and pulling rank in the close confines of the ISS where astronauts live and work cheek by jowl for a minimum of six months at a time. The hierarchy, such as it is, is therefore based on experience.

COUNTDOWN TO LIFT OFF
NASA astronauts currently use Russian Soyuz spacecraft to reach the ISS. The crew number varies but typically would be six, drawn from cosmonauts and astronauts, including international astronauts – members of the Russian, Canadian, European or Japanese space programmes who undergo NASA training and join their missions.

Chief of the Astronaut Office
Head of the Astronaut Corps. An ex-astronaut and 'father figure', and principal advisor to the NASA Administrator on training and operations, including crew assignments for missions.

Commander
A highly experienced astronaut in overall charge of a mission, responsible for the crew's safety, the spacecraft and making sure that the science on board is carried out properly and to schedule.

Pilot
Assists the commander. May also have other roles, such as undertaking EVAs (extravehicular activities – spacewalks).

Mission specialist
Specialist in and responsible for an aspect of a mission, e.g. the onboard systems, payloads, usage of consumables, education. They may also perform EVAs.

Astronaut candidate

Candidates must be US citizens from the military or they may be civilians, but they must have a bachelor's degree in engineering, maths or physical, biological or computer science, and be fit enough to pass the physical. Very few of the thousands of applicants are actually accepted. After having completed their training, and having taken part in a space flight more than 100 km (62 miles) above the Earth, new astronauts receive an astronaut pin (badge). Each service (Army, Navy, Air Force) issues their own pins featuring the astronaut device (a shooting star through a halo). Civilian astronauts receive special pins. The roles they take on as astronauts depend on their pre-NASA background, with engineers becoming mission specialists, pilots becoming commanders, and so on.

EXTRA VEHICULAR ACTIVITY (EVA)

Tech talk for the far more exciting (or terrifying) sounding layman's term spacewalk. It applies to any occasion on which an astronaut goes outside the craft when in space. Tethers attached to the spacecraft stop them floating off into the void, while a SAFER (Simplifed Aid for EVA Rescue) is a backpack that packs a jet-propelled punch to push the astronaut back to the craft in case of accidental untethering.

Chakras

Chakra is a Sanskrit word for a spinning 'wheel' of invisible energy or life force, called *prana*. There are seven main chakras, and according to Ayurvedic tradition they must remain open and aligned in order for the mind, body and soul to be healthy and in harmony. It's akin to spinning plates on poles – let one fall, and they all go awry.

The bottom three chakras are related to the physical self and the top three to the higher, or spiritual, self. The heart chakra forms a bridge between the two aspects. The chakra hierarchy appears reversed, with the first chakra at the base of the spine and the seventh – the chakra of enlightenment, the state to which followers of Eastern spiritual traditions ultimately aspire – at the crown of the head.

Muladhara
The first (root) chakra is at the base of the spine. It's associated with the colour red and relates to material stability and security.

Svadhisthana
The second (sacral) chakra sits below the navel. It's associated with the colour orange and relates to creative expression.

Manipura
The third (solar plexus) chakra lies between the navel and the breastbone. It's associated with the colour yellow and relates to personal power.

Anahata
The fourth (heart) chakra is located in the centre of the chest. It's associated with the colour green and is the source of love and connection.

Vishuddha
The fifth (throat) chakra is in the neck area. It's associated with the colour blue and relates to verbal expression.

Ajna
The sixth (third-eye) chakra sits between the eyebrows. It's associated with the colour indigo and is the centre of intuition, or sixth sense.

Sahaswara
The seventh (crown, or 'thousand petal lotus') chakra is located at the top of the head and thus is the only one not centred on the spinal column. It's associated with the colour violet and is the chakra of enlightenment and spiritual connection to the divine.

The Human Body

The human body has six associated levels of structural organisation: chemical, cellular, tissue, organ, organ system and organismal. The first, and simplest of these, includes the tiniest building blocks of matter essential for maintaining life, and the highest, the organismal level, is the sum total of all the structural levels in our bodies.

1 CHEMICAL LEVEL

Atoms: the smallest unit of matter, two or more of which combine to form a molecule.

Molecules: (e.g. water molecules, DNA, glucose) these can be simple or complex and are the chemical building blocks of life, which combine to form:

Organelles ('little organs'): specific structures that perform specific functions within the body.

2 CELLULAR LEVEL

Cells: molecules are organised into cells, the smallest units of living matter and the basic units of structure and function of life, each with a unique task in the body. Cells vary in size, shape and function (muscle cells, nerve cells, blood cells).

3 TISSUE LEVEL

Tissues: groups of similar cells are organised into tissues to perform a function (e.g. epithelial, connective, muscle and nervous tissues). Each tissue has a role in the body.

4 ORGAN LEVEL

Organs: groups of at least two types of tissue that perform a specific function (e.g. liver, stomach, heart, lungs, brain).

5 ORGAN SYSTEM LEVEL

Organ systems: groups of organs that work together to perform a common function. There are eleven organ systems in the body: integumentary, muscular, skeletal, nervous, endocrine, cardiovascular, lymphatic, respiratory, digestive, urinary, reproductive.

6 ORGANISMAL LEVEL

Organ system: the highest level of structural organisation, it consists of organ systems working together to perform a common function of the body and to keep a stable internal environment. It is the sum total of all the structural levels.

STRONG AND STABLE

The maintenance of a constant, stable and balanced internal environment is known as homeostasis ('stay the same').
An example of this is the control of the amount of carbon dioxide in the blood. Diabetes is a condition that results from the body's inability to regulate its blood glucose levels.

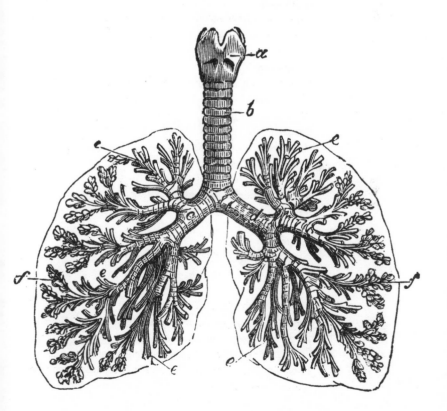

46

Ecological Hierarchy

Ecological hierarchy theory describes the relationship between biological organisms. Living things are organised into increasingly larger and complex groups. Top down they are as follows:

Biosphere
All areas where life exists, i.e. most of the Earth, including the atmosphere, a sum of all the ecosystems.

Biome
A set of ecosystems sharing similar characteristics.

Ecosystem
Living organisms and non-living aspects of the environment such as air, water, light, etc.

Community
All the populations (plants, animals, micro-organisms) in a specific area.

Population
Members of the same species living in the same area at the same time and interacting with each other.

Individual species (organism)
Basic living systems.

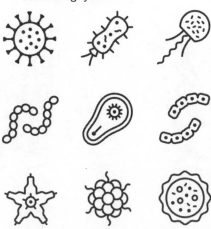

Plankton

Plankton are diverse organisms that live in water and occur in sizes ranging from a few microns to metres. They are found in oceans, seas, lakes, rivers and ponds and are traditionally divided into the following size-based categories, the prefix referring to a metric unit of measurement:

Femtoplankton (femto, meaning one quadrillionth) mostly marine viruses, less than 0.2 μm in size

Picoplankton (pico, meaning one trillionth) bacteria, cyanobacteria 0.2–2 μm

Nanoplankton (nano, meaning one billionth) flagellates, 2–20 μm

Microplankton (micro, meaning one millionth) diatoms and cillates, 20–200 μm

Mesoplankton:
zooplankton and copepods, 0.2–20mm

Macroplankton:
larvaceans, larval fishes and other zooplankton, 20–200mm

Megaplankton:
jellyfish, salps and other zooplankton, greater than 200mm

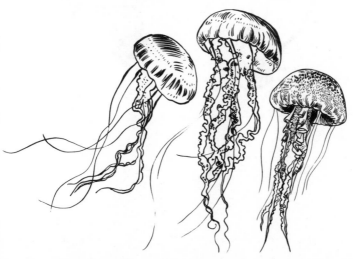

The Body Mass Index

Obesity has become a major problem in the developed world, contributing to a whole range of potentially life-threatening health issues. The Body Mass Index (BMI), a measure of body fat based on the ratio between a person's height and weight, is derived from the Quetelet Index, published in 1832 by a Belgian statistician and sociologist Adolphe Quetelet.

Although Quetelet himself had no interest in obesity, the usefulness of his index as an indicator of the condition was identified 140 years later, and from 1995, when the term was adopted by the World Health Organisation, BMI became the buzzword for flagging up the point at which plump becomes perilous. And, of course, it works both ways – anything below the lower limit of the 'normal' range is potentially dangerously underweight.

Normal	A BMI range of 18.5–24.9 is considered normal, and the range everyone should remain within to have the maximum chance of maintaining good health.
Overweight	A range of 25–29.9 is a sign that it's time to adjust the diet, step up the exercise, and shed a few kilos.
Obese	The range 30–34.9 suggests you've tipped over into hazardous territory.
Severely obese	A range of 35–39.9 means you're becoming ominously close to the peak of this hierarchy . . .
Morbidly obese	A BMI of 40 or above is considered literally life-threatening.
	However, it is becoming increasingly apparent that BMI as an indicator of obesity as a health risk is not foolproof, partly because it assumes that everyone has exactly the same proportion of fat, muscle and bone, but also because it does not take account of where in the body the fat is stored. There are two possibilities, and one is far more dangerous than the other:
Subcutaneous obesity	This is where the fat is stored just under the skin. If you're going to store fat, hope for this low-risk type.
Visceral obesity	The fat is stored internally, particularly around the abdominal organs, and it's the high-risk type. A high waist-to-hip ratio is believed to be a telltale sign that this is where fat is lurking.

BIG, MUSCLY INDIVIDUALS
Professional male rugby players are big, solid individuals, whose bulk is composed entirely of muscle – but based on the BMI, most would be classed overweight, if not clinically obese, highlighting the flaws in the system.

Don't Sugar the Pill

Whichever way you look at it, excess sugar is bad for you. It can result in not just visits to the dentist but weight gain and other health complications. Ranking the products that deliver sweetness in order of 'least bad if you insist on having it' is not clear cut and the list (not exhaustive, starting with least bad) we offer here would be disputed by some experts. Most of the products are still high in sugar so while some contain small amounts of minerals or nutrients (which you can also get from other food), it makes them only slightly 'less bad' than sugar. And no matter how healthy nectar and honey may sound, they are still sugar, with all the accompanying health implications. Still, most people will perceive some benefit from replacing sugar with a 'less bad' alternative, providing they don't use it as an excuse to add sugar to their diet.

The difference between the products here is really pretty minimal and the advice is normally to limit sugar intake without avoiding it altogether.

NB The list is not exhaustive – other sugars are available!

Stevia

A natural sweetener from the leaves of the stevia plant and produced as a powder or liquid. It is around two hundred times sweeter than sugar but is sugar-free, contains no calories and won't impact on blood glucose levels. Counterintuitively, it leaves a slightly bitter aftertaste. As it is heat-stable, it can be used in cooking as a sugar replacement.

Xylitol

A sweetener that is found naturally in small amounts in fruit and vegetables but can also be produced artificially. It belongs to a group known as sugar alcohols and although it contains some carbohydrate it contains fewer calories and has a lesser effect on blood sugar levels than sucrose. Studies indicate it has some benefits for dental health (it is often used in chewing gum and oral products), but don't overdo it, in quantity it can have a laxative effect.

Honey

Raw honey contains some beneficial properties (anti-microbial and anti-bacterial). Regular honey is filtered and pasteurised to prevent it from crystallising, but it loses some nutrients and vitamins in the process. Honey is sweeter than sugar and is still high in calories. Honey should not be given to infants as it can cause infant botulism.

Pure maple syrup
(light to dark)

This contains some nutrients, but is high in sugar. Don't confuse with *maple-flavoured* corn syrup, which is usually higher in calories and lower in nutrients.

Molasses

A thick liquid produced after sugar is extracted from sugar cane – several extractions are made, the first is lighter in colour, contains more sugar and so is sweeter than the third, blackstrap molasses, although blackstrap contains more vitamins and minerals. But molasses is still high in sugar.

Coconut sugar

From the sap of the coconut palm. The sap is extracted and then dried. It has some nutrient content but is about as high in calories as regular sugar.

Raw cane sugar

From the sugar cane plant, it is less refined than white sugar ... but it is still sugar and is high in calories.

Brown sugar
(light to dark)

White sugar to which molasses has been added after the refining process. It contains a very small amount of nutrients but has the same number of calories as white sugar.

Sucrose/table sugar	From sugar cane or sugar beet. It is 50:50 glucose and fructose. Highly refined and processed as white sugar, it would be incorrect to say that it has no nutritional value whatsoever as it does contain calories, and calories provide energy. But it is high in those calories and has no nutritional value beyond them.
Corn syrup/high-fructose corn syrup (HFCS)	Produced from cornstarch and used in many foods, HFCS in particular has come in for criticism due to its high fructose content (see health issues below). It has no nutritional value but delivers the same level of sweetness as sugar (contrary to popular belief) and is high in calories.
Agave nectar/syrup	Refined from the sap of the blue agave plant. It has a low GI (around 20) but is high in fructose (more than regular sugar), so when consumed in large amounts may cause health problems (see below). All the beneficial properties of the plant are destroyed during the refining process.

GLUCOSE V. FRUCTOSE
Glucose (aka dextrose) is found in many healthy foods. Virtually every cell in the body can metabolise glucose to give us energy, while the liver is the only organ that can metabolise significant amounts of fructose. Concerns have been raised that a higher intake of fructose has been linked to fatty liver disease, diabetes, cancer and heart disease, although the research is far from being substantiated.

SWEET ENOUGH?
As artificial sweeteners (most are produced chemically) are much sweeter than sugar and contain no or fewer calories (but also no nutrients), they are often used to help control weight. Some are subject to investigation regarding side effects to health and some studies are ongoing. Two examples: Aspartame (E951), 180–200 times sweeter than sugar. Questions have been raised about its potential effects on health, although many authorities have now found it safe. Those with the rare condition phenylketonuria (PKU) should, however, avoid it or take advice. Saccharin, around 300 times sweeter than sugar and often used in low-calorie food and drinks. Also investigated in the past for side effects on health, it is now permitted in processed food and drink at certain levels.

50

The Solar UV Index

Sunlight is an important source of vitamin D, made in the body when bare skin is exposed to sunlight; but, exposing fair skin to sunlight can result in cancer. To help us take advantage of the former while avoiding the latter, the World Health Organisation, the United Nations Environment Programme and the World Meteorological Organisation collaborated to develop a UV Index (UVI), a measure of the level of harmful ultraviolet radiation, usually at its highest around solar noon.

The higher the number on the UVI, the greater the potential for skin and eyes to be damaged, and the faster that damage will occur. The numbers are represented in colour, ranging from 'safe' green to 'dangerous' violet, to provide instant recognition on weather charts showing forecast ultraviolet levels.

ELEVATED UVI
On 29 December 2003, a mind-blowing UVI of 43 was recorded in the Bolivian Andes of South America. The high elevation of the region, combined with the midday sun, is expected to produce high levels, but this measurement took 'extreme' to extremes.

Low

UVI 1 and 2 (green)
You can safely stay outside.

Moderate

UVI 3, 4 and 5 (yellow)

High

UVI 6 and 7 (orange)
Seek shade during midday hours. Slip on a shirt, slop on sunscreen and slap on a hat:

Very high

UVI 8, 9 and 10 (red)

Extreme

UVI 11+ (violet)
Avoid being outside during midday hours. Make sure you seek shade. Shirt, sunscreen and hat are a must: Bright reflective surfaces and white sand can double UV exposure.

The Beaufort Wind Force Scale

Developed in 1805 by British hydrographer Rear Admiral Sir Francis Beaufort, the scale is used to describe wind intensity on land and sea through observable conditions rather than precise measurements. Running from 0 (calm) to 12 (hurricane), it is the wind measurement scale most widely used today.

Beaufort Number	Wind speed (knots per hour)	Description	Wave height (in feet)	Sea	Land
0	less than 1	Calm	0	Flat	Smoke rises vertically
1	1–2	Light air	0.33	Ripples	Wind moves smoke
2	3–6	Light breeze	0.66	Small wavelets that do not break	Wind can be felt on skin; leaves rustle
3	7–10	Gentle breeze	2	Large wavelets; some cresting	Leaves and smaller twigs in motion
4	11–15	Moderate breeze	3.3	Small waves	Dust and paper dance; small branches move
5	16–20	Fresh breeze	6.6	Moderate waves; some foam and spray	Moderate branches and small trees sway
6	21–26	Strong breeze	9.9	Large waves, foaming crests, spray	Large branches sway; wind whistles through wires; bins fall over
7	27–33	High wind, moderate gale	13.1	Water heaps up, foaming streaks	Trees move; hard to walk against the wind; tall buildings sway
8	34–40	Fresh gale	18	Moderate high waves, breaking crests, spray	Twigs break off trees; vehicles blown off course
9	41–47	Strong gale	23	High waves, dense foam	Larger branches and small trees break or blow over; damage to fences; tents blow down
10	48–55	Whole gale/storm	29.5	Very high waves, large patches of boiling foam, much airborne spray	Trees broken off or uprooted; tiles blow off roofs
11	56–63	Violent storm	37.7	Exceptionally high waves, very large foam patches, airborne spray reducing visibility	Trees uprooted; roofs damaged, or blown off
12	64 plus	Hurricane	46 plus	Huge waves, entire sea white with foam, airborne spray reduces visibility to nothing.	Widespread damage to vegetation and structures; airborne debris

The Richter Scale

In 1935, Charles F. Richter of the California Institute of Technology developed his eponymous magnitude scale as a mathematical device for comparing the size of earthquakes. It used a formula based on the amplitude of the largest wave of energy as recorded by a seismograph, with adjustments made for the distance between the epicentre and the location of the various seismographs. The Richter scale has a base-10 logarithmic scale and is expressed in whole numbers with decimal fractions. Each whole number represents a tenfold increase in amplitude and the release of 31.7 times as much energy.

San Francisco's 'Great Quake' in 1906 left almost 80 per cent of the city damaged and was given a 7.8 rating. The largest quake ever recorded was a magnitude 9.5 in Chile on 22 May 1960. A 10 is thought to be impossible. The Richter scale does not provide accurate estimates for large magnitude earthquakes and was succeeded in the 1970s by the moment magnitude scale (abbreviated as MW), which is preferred today, and measures an earthquake in terms of the energy released.

EARTHQUAKE MAGNITUDE CLASS

Class	Magnitude
Great	8.0–8.9 and 9.0 or more

Felt across extremely large regions; severe damage to or total destruction of structures, including earthquake-resistant buildings. Honshu, Japan, 2011, 9.0.

Major	7.0–7.9

Felt across great distances; collapse of/damage to many buildings within around 240 km (150 miles) of the epicentre. Kathmandu, Nepal, 2015, 7.8.

Strong	6.0–6.9

Felt up to hundreds of miles from the epicentre, strong/violent shaking in the epicentre; damage to well-constructed buildings, some damage to earthquake-resistant buildings. Northridge, California, 1994, 6.8.

Moderate   5.0–5.9

Possible slight damage to well-constructed buildings.
Ontario–Quebec border, Canada, 2010, 5.0.

Light   4.0–4.9

Noticeable shaking of indoor objects; usually only minimal
damage.

Minor   2.0–2.9 and 3.0–3.9

Felt by humans if they are near the epicentre; rarely causes
damage.

Micro-earthquake   1.0–1.9

Barely felt by humans.

53

The Saffir-Simpson Hurricane Wind Scale

A hurricane is defined as a storm with a violent wind, in particular a tropical cyclone in the Caribbean. To be classed as a hurricane, the wind speed must be force 12 on the Beaufort Scale (see page 80) – that is, equal to or exceeding 119 km (74 miles/64 knots) per hour. People living in the hurricane belt have to be constantly on their toes, as the transition from a relatively innocent tropical depression to a 'named storm' to a hurricane is often very rapid. The US National Oceanic and Atmospheric Administration (NOAA) National Hurricane Center even organises an annual 'hurricane preparedness week' before the season starts, with daily tasks to be carried out, from 'Determine your risk' to 'Complete your written hurricane plan'.

Developed in the 1970s by Herbert Saffir and Robert Simpson, the Saffir-Simpson Hurricane Wind Scale is based on a hurricane's sustained wind speed, defined as speed sustained for over one minute:

STORM GOD

The word 'hurricane' comes from the Spanish huracán, thought to derive from the Taino god of storm, Hurakán. It was coined in the sixteenth century, when Spanish settlers were busy colonising the Caribbean area.

1 Wind speed 119–153 km/h (74–95 mph; 64–82 kt/h)

Very dangerous; winds will produce some damage. Category 1 Hurricane Stan caused 3.96 billion dollars' worth of damage and 1,668 deaths in Mexico and Central America in 2005.

2 Wind speed 154–177 km/h (96–110 mph; 83–95 kt/h)

Extremely dangerous; winds will cause extensive damage. The charmingly named but decidedly vicious Fife-Orlene caused 1.8 billion dollars' worth of damage and 8,000 deaths in Jamaica, Mexico and Central America in 1974.

3 Wind speed 178–208 km/h (111–129 mph; 96–112 kt/h)

Devastating damage will occur. The costliest (and third deadliest) US hurricane, Katrina, was a mere category 3 – but it still managed to inflict over 108 billion dollars' worth of damage to property, particularly in the New Orleans area. The exact death toll is uncertain but figures between 1,200 and 1,836 were reported.

4 Wind speed 209–251 km/h (130–156 mph; 113–136 kt/h)

Catastrophic damage will occur. The storm with the highest death toll in the USA was the category 4 Great Galveston Hurricane of 1900, which caused an estimated loss of life of between 8,000 and 12,000. At this rating (and 5) most of the area will be uninhabitable for weeks or months.

5 Wind speed 252 km/h (157 mph/137 kt) or higher

Catastrophic damage will occur. The record for the highest recorded wind speed at landfall is held by the 1969 category 5 hurricane Camille, at an estimated 190 miles per hour when it struck the US Mississippi coast.

NAME AND NUMBER

Storms (force 10 and 11 on the Beaufort scale) and hurricanes are given short, distinctive names for the purpose of unambiguous identification and communication when two or more storms are raging at the same time, often hundreds of miles apart. The system of using female names for storms began in 1953 and continued until 1978 (for the Northern Pacific) and 1979 (for the Atlantic basin), when male names were added. The list of names for Atlantic hurricanes is used on a six-year rotation, and a name is only dropped when it has been used for a particularly significant storm in terms of fatalities or cost.

Sea States

The general state of the surface of a large body of water varies with the prevailing conditions. Determined by wave height, frequency and power, it can be measured using instruments such as wave radar and weather buoys, or assessed visually by an experienced observer.

0 Calm (glassy)
0 metres (0 ft)

1 Calm (rippled)
0 to 0.1 metres (0.00 to 0.33 ft)

2 Smooth (wavelets)
0.1 to 0.5 metres (3.9 in to 1 ft 7.7 in)

3 Slight
0.5 to 1.25 metres (1 ft 8 in to 4 ft 1 in)

4 Moderate
1.25 to 2.5 metres (4 ft 1 in to 8 ft 2 in)

5 Rough
2.5 to 4 metres (8 ft 2 in to 13 ft 1 in)

6 Very rough
4 to 6 metres (13 to 20 ft)

7 High
6 to 9 metres (20 to 30 ft)

8 Very high
9 to 14 metres (30 to 46 ft)

9 Phenomenal
Over 14 metres (46 ft)

Icebergs

Icebergs form when chunks of ice break away from glaciers or ice shelves – a process known as 'calving' – in Arctic and Antarctic regions. Once calved, the iceberg drifts into more temperate waters and starts to erode and break up. Although it might be expected that the prosaically named 'very large' category poses the biggest threat to shipping, it is in fact the smaller and more interestingly named bergy bits and growlers that are far more dangerous as they are harder to spot. The most famous iceberg in history is the one the liner *Titanic* collided with on her maiden voyage in 1912. As a result, the International Ice Patrol (IIP), operated by the United States Coast Guard, was established the following year to keep North Atlantic shipping informed of potential danger and eliminate risk of collision. IIP categories are as follows:

Very large berg
More than 75 m (240 ft) in height; more than 204 m (670 ft) in length.

Large berg
46–75 m (151–240 ft) in height; 123–204 m (401–670 ft) in length.

Medium berg
16–45 m (51–150 ft) in height; 61–122 m (201–400 ft) in length.

Small berg
5–15 m (14–50 ft) in height; 15–60 (47–200 ft) in length.

Bergy bit
1–4 m (3–13 ft) in height; 5–14 m (15–46 ft) in length.

Growler
Less than 1 m (3 ft) in height; less than 5 m (16 ft) in length.

A CUT ABOVE
The world's largest recorded iceberg, known as B-15, was nearly 300 km (186 miles) long and 40 km (25 miles) wide (that's a staggering 300,000 m/982,080 ft long and 37,000 m/132,000 ft wide), leaving no shred of doubt as to which category it fell into. It calved from the Ross Ice Shelf in Antarctica in March 2000; satellite imagery revealed that a fragment of the berg was still drifting thirteen years later.

Australian Bushfires

Bushfires have been a part of the landscape in Australia for millions of years. They occur regularly in the hotter months in both mountainous and flat regions, in forested areas, grass, scrub or bush. The Australian FDR (Fire Danger Rating) was adopted by all the country's states in 2009 and is based on forecast weather conditions from the Bureau of Meteorology. Advice is given about the level of threat on a particular day. The fires usually occur during periods of high temperature, low humidity and strong winds, and can be devastating. The Black Saturday bushfire of 2009 in Victoria destroyed over 2,000 homes, with 173 fatalities.

0–11 Low to Moderate & 12–31 High

Fires are likely to be controlled under these conditions and homes can provide safety. Bushfire survival plans should be checked.

32–49 Very High

Fires could be difficult to control by firefighters in these conditions, which are likely to be hot, dry and possibly windy. Well-prepared and well-defended homes can provide safety, with vital equipment including a water supply, a petrol/diesel portable pump, a generator and protective clothing.

50–74 Severe & 75–99 Extreme

In hot, dry and windy conditions fires that take hold move quickly, and are unpredictable and difficult for firefighters to bring under control. Spot fires are likely to start and spread quickly. Only homes with bushfire protection and active defences may provide safety. Equipment required is as for the previous category, and fire risk areas should be left early in the day. The only safe place is away from bushfire risk areas.

100+ Catastrophic

The worst conditions for bushfires. If a fire starts and takes hold, firefighters find it extremely difficult to control. Spot fires start ahead of the main fire and cause the fire to spread rapidly. The only safe place is away from bushfire risk areas. Immediate action is required.

Nuclear Event

INES (the International Nuclear and Radiological Event Scale) rates any event associated with the use, storage and transport of radioactive material and radiation sources. Its purpose is to ensure that nuclear authorities, the public and media understand an event's 'safety significance'. Events are rated over seven levels; the severity increases approximately ten times with each increase in level, which looks at three categories of impact: people and the environment, radiological barriers and control (unplanned high radiation levels inside facilities), and defence-in-depth (protection measures that did not function as intended).

INCIDENT

Level 1 Anomaly
Overexposure of a member of the public in excess of the statutory annual limits; minor problems with safety components.

Level 2 Incident
Atucha, Argentina, 2005; Cadarache, France, 1993; Forsmark, Sweden, 2006.

Significant contamination within a facility into an area not expected by design; exposure of workers in excess of the statutory annual limits, exposure of a member of the public in excess of 10 mSv (millisieverts – radiation is generally measured in sieverts, after the Swedish physicist Rolf Maximilian Sievert.

Level 3 Serious incident
Sellafield, UK, 2005; Vandellos, Spain, 1989.

Exposure in excess of ten times the statutory annual limit for workers. Non-lethal health effect. Severe contamination in an area not expected by design, low probability of significant public exposure.

Level 4 Accident with local consequences

Tokaimura, Japan, 1999; Saint Laurent des Eaux, France, 1980.

Minor release of radioactive material, unlikely to require implementation of countermeasures other than food controls; at least one death from radiation. Release of significant quantities of radioactive material within an installation, significant public exposure highly likely.

Level 5 Accident with wider consequences

Three-Mile Island, USA, 1979; Windscale Piles, UK, 1957.

Limited release of radioactive material likely to require implementation of countermeasures; several deaths from radiation. Severe damage to reactor core; large quantities of radioactive material released within an installation, significant public exposure highly likely.

Level 6 Serious accident

Kyshtym, Russia, 1957.

Significant release of radioactive material likely to require implementation of countermeasures.

Level 7 Major accident

Chernobyl, Ukraine, 1986; Fukushima, Japan, 2011.

Major release of radioactive material; widespread effects on health and the environment requiring implementation of planned and extended countermeasures.

Events with no safety significance are not rated.

NB The above exclude the INES Defence-in-Depth rating except for Level 1.

DEFCON

This famous ranking system with its attention-grabbing alternative names describes the defence readiness of US military forces to deal with the perceived threat to national security. It was first mapped out in 1959.

Defcon 1 (Cocked Pistol or White Alert)
'Maximum Defense Readiness Condition' – nuclear war imminent. This level has never been implemented.

Defcon 2 (Fast Pace or Red Alert)
The armed forces are ready to be deployed in 6 hours or less. This level was reached in the Cuban Missile Crisis in 1962.

Defcon 3 (Round House or Yellow Alert)
A state of military readiness.

Defcon 4 (Double Take or Green Alert)
Security is strengthened and intel gathered.

Defcon 5 (Fade Out or Blue Alert)
A state of peace, no immediate need to be on alert.

TERRORIST THREAT IN THE USA

The five-colour alert system (from green to red) instigated in the USA by the Bush administration in 2002 after the attacks of 9/11 was deemed too vague, scaring rather than preparing people for action. It was replaced in 2011 by a simple two-tier system devised by the National Terrorism Advisory System (NTAS). The alert is issued for a specific period only.

Imminent threat alert
A credible, specific and impending terrorist threat against the United States.

Elevated threat alert
A credible terrorist threat against the United States.

By the 1950s, alert systems to protect the UK's civilian population had moved on considerably from beacons lit on headlands to warn of the approach of a foreign (and probably hostile) fleet and acoustic mirrors (large concrete reflectors), a kind of primitive radar of the 1920s.

HANDEL

In the Cold War a system code-named HANDEL was ready to warn the general public of attack. It made use of the network used by the speaking clock to activate sirens countrywide. This may sound rather low-tech but was in fact, a smart move profiting from the fact that the network was already in existence and any faults on it would automatically be picked up quickly. HANDEL was developed in 1962 and was decommissioned in the early 1990s.

BIKINI state alert

A colour-coded system in use between 1970 and 2006. It warned of non-specific threats including civil disorder and war as well as terrorism. It was used by government departments only and ran from **white** (situation stable) through **black** (possibility of attack), **black special** (increased likelihood), **amber** (substantial threat) to **red** (information received about a specific target).

TERRORIST THREAT IN THE UK TODAY

The JTAC (Joint Terrorism Analysis Centre) and the Security Service MI5 assess the likelihood of a terrorist attack in the UK, analysing information from the police, government departments and agencies. They take into account the intelligence available, knowledge of terrorist intentions and capabilities, and timescale. There are five levels of threat and they can change at any time:

Low
An attack is unlikely.

Moderate
An attack is possible, but not likely.

Substantial
An attack is a strong possibility.

Severe
An attack is highly likely.

Critical
An attack is expected imminently.

Dante's Circles of Hell

According to Italian poet Dante, who was given a tour of the place by Virgil, Hell consists of a vestibule followed by nine circles of suffering, subdivided by three rivers, boring deep into the underworld and centred on Satan, trapped in ice at the centre of the Earth. It is encircled by a Dark Wood, patrolled by a lion, a leopard and a she-wolf. The circles are concentric, each being reserved for a specific sin, which increase in wickedness as the centre of the Earth is approached, culminating in betrayal. The deeper it goes, the more complicated the architecture. Dante described it in detail in The Inferno, a section of his long three-part narrative poem *The Divine Comedy*, completed in 1370 and published in 1432.

VESTIBULE

Sinners
The uncommitted, don't-knows and opportunists.

Punishment
To run forever in fog, flowing with blood and pus and covered in maggots, and pursued by swarms of wasps and hornets.

River Acheron

UPPER HELL
CIRCLE

FIRST
Limbo.

Sinners
The unbaptised, virtuous pagans; includes large numbers of classical poets and philosophers, and Virgil himself.

Punishment
Eternity spent in a castle representing an inferior form of heaven.

CIRCLE

SECOND

Sinners
The lustful.

Punishment
Constantly buffeted by violent winds and terrible storms in pitch dark.

CIRCLE	THIRD

Sinners
The gluttons.

Punishment
Blinded and forced to wallow in icy putrescent sludge and flayed by the claws of Cerberus if they try to get out.

CIRCLE	FOURTH

Sinners
The greedy, misers, profligates, hoarders and spendthrifts.

Punishment
Smothered in heavy weights and forced to fight by rolling over and crushing each other.

River Styx

CIRCLE	FIFTH

Sinners
The angry.

Punishment
The Styx runs through this circle forming the Stygian swamp. The enraged fight each other in the slime, while the passive-aggressive lie under the mud to putrefy.

The City of Dis, the entrance to Lower Hell. Guarded by fallen angels.

LOWER HELL

CIRCLE | **SIXTH**

Sinners
Heretics.

Punishment
Crammed into burning tombs.

CIRCLE | **SEVENTH**
This circle, the designated abode of the violent, is guarded by the Minotaur and is divided into three separate rings.

RING ONE
Sinners
Those violent against their neighbours: warmongers, murderers, tyrants and plunderers.

Punishment
Immersed in the Phlegethon, a river of boiling blood and fire; the more violent they were in life, the deeper they plunge. Armed centaurs patrol the banks and shoot anyone who tries to get out.

RING TWO
Sinners
Those violent against themselves; suicides.

Punishment
Transformed into gnarled trees in the Wood of Suicides, where they are pecked by Harpies.

RING THREE
Sinners
Those violent against art, nature and God; blasphemers, sodomites and usurers.

Punishment
Stranded on the burning hot sands of a great desert, tormented by flakes of fire that fall like rain. Blasphemers are forced to lie on their backs on the sand; sodomites are forced to run constantly in circles; usurers crouch and weep constantly.

The River Phlegethon forms a waterfall that leads down to the Eighth Circle.

CIRCLE

EIGHTH
Malebolge

This circle is divided into ten concentric trenches (bolge) and is shaped like an amphitheatre.

TRENCH ONE
Sinners

Panderers and seducers.

Punishment

March around the ditch continuously, while being whipped by horned demons.

TRENCH TWO
Sinners

Flatterers.

Punishment

Immersed in excrement.

TRENCH THREE
Sinners

Simoniacs: people who sold ecclesiastical office and preferment.

Punishment

Rammed head first into narrow font-like holes in the rock and burned on soles of feet.

TRENCH FOUR
Sinners

Magicians, diviners, astrologers, false prophets.

Punishment

Heads twisted 180 degrees and forced to walk backwards.

TRENCH FIVE
Sinners

Corrupt politicians.

Punishment

Immersed in a lake of boiling pitch; tormented by malebranche, demons with claws and grappling hooks, if they try to get out.

TRENCH SIX
Sinners
Hypocrites.

Punishment
Forced to walk perpetually wearing lead-lined gilded robes.

TRENCH SEVEN
Sinners
Thieves.

Punishment
Trapped in a pit of biting reptiles, snakes and lizards; repeatedly consumed by fire.

TRENCH EIGHT
Sinners
Counsellors of fraud; people who advise others to be fraudulent; evil éminences grises.

Punishment
Constantly encased in flame.

TRENCH NINE
Sinners
Sowers of discord in the family, the community or religious matters.

Punishment
Repeatedly hacked to pieces by a huge demon with a sword.

TRENCH TEN
Sinners
Falsifiers: alchemists, impostors, counterfeiters, liars.

Punishment
In constant darkness, afflicted with hideous diseases.

In the centre of Malebolge is the well that leads down to the bottom-most Circle.

CIRCLE

NINTH

At the bottom of this circle is Cocytus, the lake of ice, the abode of traitors. It is divided into four concentric lanes.

Lane 1 Caina
Sinners
Traitors to family and kindred.

Punishment
Frozen up to neck in ice, but can move their head.

Lane 2 Antenora
Sinners
Traitors to country.

Punishment
Frozen up to chin in ice, but can move their head.

Lane 3 Ptolomea
Sinners
Traitors to guests.

Punishment
Stretched out on their backs on the ice, their tears freezing their eyeballs.

Lane 4 Judecca
Sinners
Traitors to lords and benefactors.

Punishment
Their entire body immersed in the ice.

Satan is trapped up to his waist in the centre of the lake. He has three faces and gnaws on a traitor in each mouth. Julius Caesar's assassins are being eternally consumed, Brutus on the left and Cassius on the right, while treacherous apostle Judas Iscariot is in the centre.

Typography

The way type is organised helps establish the importance of the information being presented. It guides the reader's eye, allowing them to navigate content easily, signalling the beginnings and ends of text and picking out important data. Typographic hierarchy is unusual in that the most important item in a document may not be positioned at the top and the hierarchy is fluid, changing according to the design of the document or text.

The tools most commonly used for typographic styling are listed below. They can be used in any combination by a skilled and creative graphic designer, but a conventional and fairly obvious hierarchy would be:

Size	The most obvious way of demonstrating importance.
Weight	Using a heavier (i.e. bolder/thicker) font.
Colour	A useful way of picking out type. Warm colours (reds, oranges) generally shout out at us while blues and greens recede more against a white background, for example.
Contrasting font	Different typefaces also add emphasis.
Position	Where type is positioned in a document also affects emphasis, drawing the eye.
Spacing	Type in isolation, for example, may stand out more.

A CONVENTIONAL DESIGN MAY AIM FOR THREE LEVELS

LEVEL ONE
The most important content should be the most immediately visible.
In a newspaper article, this could be a headline.

Level two
The text should be organised into clear sections so the reader can easily navigate to the part they want.
In a newspaper, a subheading.

Level three
The substance of the document should be easy to read.
In a newspaper, the text of the article.

Tolkien's Rings of Power

J. R. R. Tolkien's epic *The Lord of the Rings* (1953/4) focuses on the quest to destroy the One Ring of Power and Sauron, its evil creator, but there are twenty rings in the story. Sauron, in disguise, helped to make sixteen of them with Celebrimbor the Elven Smith, intending to give them to Dwarves and Men to keep them in his power. Celebrimbor alone made the three Elven rings. Sauron forged the One Ring that he thought ruled them all.

THE ONE RING

Gold. No stone.
Elven script of an incantation in the Black Speech of Mordor, visible only when the ring is put in fire.

Powers: bends all others to its will; can make the wearer invisible and prolong their life.

Worn by: Sauron, Isildur, Gollum (Sméagol), Bilbo Baggins, Frodo Baggins.

THE THREE ELVEN RINGS

Vilya
Gold with a blue stone/sapphire.
Also known as the Ring of Air, the Ring of Firmament, the Blue Ring.

Powers: healing, control of the elements.

Worn by: Elrond, Elf Lord of Rivendell.

Narya
Gold with a red stone/ruby.
Also known as Narya the Great, the Ring of Fire, the Red Ring and The Kindler.

Powers: resistance to evil, inspiring hope in others.

Worn by: Gandalf the Wizard.

Nenya
Mithril (silver) with a white stone/diamond.
Also known as Ring of Water, Ring of Adamant, the White Ring.

Powers: protection and preservation from evil.

Worn by: Galadriel, the Elf Queen of Lothlórien.

THE SEVEN RINGS   These rings have no individual names.

Powers: intensifies the darkside of the dwarf mind, leading to an obsession with amassing gold.

Worn by: the Chief of each of the dwarf clans: Longbeards (Durin's Folk), Firebeards, Broadbeams, Ironfists, Stiffbeards, Blacklocks, Stonefoots.

These rings all have equal power. Four were destroyed by dragons, and three taken back under torture by Sauron.

THE NINE RINGS   These were made by Sauron for men who had already gone to the darkside. Only the Witch King of Angmar is named in Tolkien's work.

Powers: bends the wearer to the will of Sauron.

Worn by: the Nine Riders, also known as the Ring Wraiths and the Nazgûl.

All were destroyed when the One Ring was destroyed in the fires of Mount Doom.

63

Cabinet Ministers in Her Majesty's Government

There is no established order of precedence among UK Cabinet ministers, it is decided by the Prime Minister in office at the time. But certain positions always rank highly, including the so-called Great Offices of State – the Home Secretary, the Foreign Secretary and the Chancellor. Even so, the perceived order can still be turned on its head, such as in Tony Blair's government, when Peter Mandelson had more of the PM's ear than might have been expected from his position as first Trade and Industry and subsequently Northern Ireland Secretary. A fairly conventional cabinet ranking would be, from the top job down:

Prime Minister, First Lord of the Treasury and Minister for the Civil Service

Deputy Prime Minister (not always appointed)

Chancellor of the Exchequer

Secretary of State for the Home Department

Secretary of State for Foreign and Commonwealth Affairs

Secretary of State for Defence

Lord Chancellor and Secretary of State for Justice

Secretary of State for Education

Secretary of State for Work and Pensions

Secretary of State for Health

Secretary of State for International Trade and President of the Board of Trade

Secretary of State for Business, Energy and Industrial Strategy

Secretary of State for Transport

Secretary of State for Communities and Local Government

Lord President of the Council and Leader of the House of Commons

Leader of the House of Lords and Lord Privy Seal

Secretary of State for Scotland

Secretary of State for Wales

Secretary of State for Northern Ireland

Secretary of State for Environment, Food and Rural Affairs

Secretary of State for International Development

Secretary of State for Culture, Media and Sport

Chancellor of the Duchy of Lancaster

Not forgetting any ad hoc appointments that may be necessary to deal with changing political circumstances, such as 2016's appointment of the Secretary of State for Exiting the European Union.

RANKING IN GOVERNMENT DEPARTMENTS

Cabinet Minister
A government department is headed by a secretary of state. Large/important departments, such as the Treasury, may have a second cabinet minister.

Minister of State (one to three ministers, depending on the size of the department)
Experienced ministers who assist cabinet ministers with or handle complex or politically tricky issues.

Parliamentary Under-Secretary of State
(one to four under-secretaries)
Junior ministers who perform a wide range of representational and other duties, including guiding bills through parliament.

Civil servants (any number)
Their role is to help ministers achieve their goals: through advice, helping to promote and defend the minister's decisions (even if the civil servants advised against them), seeing that the minister's decisions are implemented.

THE DEVOLUTION EFFECT
Due to the devolution of power for some aspects of government to separate assemblies in Scotland, Wales and Northern Ireland, not all departments (e.g. health, education) cover the whole of the UK.

Under its constitution (the *Grundgesetz*, or Basic Law),
Germany has a federal system of government. The
Bundestag (Federal Assembly – the lower house) and the
Bundesrat (Federal Council – the upper house) are the
government's two legislative chambers. The Bundestag
is Germany's parliament, staffed by local representatives
elected by the people, and meets in the Reichstag building
in Berlin. The Bundesrat represents Germany's sixteen
states; its function is largely advisory but some legislation
(e.g. constitutional changes) requires its consent.

Bundespräsident

The president of Germany. A largely symbolic head of
state, elected for a five-year term by secret ballot, with one
renewal.

Bundestagspräsident

The president of the Bundestag. Elected from Bundestag
members (around six hundred), he/she is in charge of
parliamentary procedure, similar to the speaker in other
nations' governments.

Bundeskanzler

The chancellor. Head of the government, elected by the
Bundestag.

Bundesratspräsident

The president of the Bundesrat (Germany's Federal Council).
Elected for one year from among the heads of the German
states (Länder), the presidency traditionally rotates between
each of them in turn.

Präsident des Bundesverfassungsgerichts

The president of the Federal Constitutional Court,
which sits in Karlsruhe, at a deliberate remove from the
other governmental bodies in Berlin. The court deals
with constitutional issues and has the power to declare
legislation unconstitutional.

Bundeskabinett

The cabinet, comprising the chancellor and the federal ministers who formulate and implement policy for their various departments. The president appoints the ministers based on proposals made by the chancellor. The cabinet includes the Vizekanzler (vice chancellor), who also serves as a federal minister.

A SERIES OF FIRSTS

Angela Merkel was born in 1954 in Hamburg, Germany, but moved to communist East Germany (known then as the GDR, or German Democratic Republic) with her family just months later. She became the first woman to chair the CDU (Christian Democratic Union) party in 2000 and is the first woman to lead Germany as chancellor.

65

Communist Party of the Soviet Union (CPSU)

The CPSU was created by members of the Bolshevik wing of the Russian Social Democratic Workers' Party (RSDWP) led by Vladimir Lenin after the Russian Revolution of October 1917. It held power until 1991 when the Soviet Union broke up under its last General Secretary, Mikhail Gorbachev. At its peak, the CPSU had around nineteen million members.

Although in many people's minds the Communist Party and the Soviet government were one and the same thing, in practice they were two separate entities and it was the CPSU that governed. The Party's structure paralleled that of government, so that at each level (province, district, city) the government official had an equivalent in the party, but the Party official's status was superior and most of the high-ranking government officials were also Party members.

Party Congress

The CPSU's governing body, which initially met annually (subsequently less frequently) and was attended by several thousand delegates. It elected the members of the Central Committee, which governed between congresses. The Congress was the supreme power until the General Secretary gradually took over the top spot – a change that began in 1922 when Stalin was elected General Secretary and by the end of the decade had become virtual dictator.

Central Auditing Commission
Elected by and reported to the Party Congress, the Commission had a supervisory role, monitoring the handling of affairs by the Party's central bodies and the Central Committee, and auditing the treasury's accounts.

Central Committee

With around three hundred members (by the 1980s), the Central Committee met twice a year and handled party administration as opposed to policy. It elected the members of the various committees, including the Politburo and the Secretariat in theory, although in practice both elected their own members.

Central Control Commission

Elected by the Central Committee of which it was a part, the Commission supervised the discipline of Party members, handing out punishments and issuing expulsions.

| **General Secretary** | Known as First Secretary 1952–66. The General Secretary was de facto head of the Politburo, from among whose members he was elected. Under Stalin it became the most powerful position in the Party and synonymous with first, Party leader, and later, leader of the whole Soviet Union. |

| **Politburo (Political bureau)** | Known as the Presidium 1952–66, it had around fifteen full members. The highest policy-making body (both domestic and foreign), the Politburo eventually overshadowed the Central Committee. Although theoretically elected by the Central Committee, in reality the Politburo elected its own members, who for most of its existence included the minister of defence, the foreign minister and the chairman of the KGB. |

| **Secretariat** | The Secretariat oversaw the administration of the regional governments and the police, army and KGB, and helped develop policy for the Politburo. Its different departments were headed by Secretaries. |

Below the Secretariat, the Party was organised, and wielded power, via a series of conferences and committees at republic (state), province (oblast) and district (raion) levels, right down to the smallest unit of all, the primary Party organisation:

| **Primary Party organisation** | Otherwise known as the Party cell. Any organisation (farm, factory, school, and so on) that contained at least three Party members could form a Party cell. |

YOUTHFUL ENTHUSIASM

Theoretically independent of the CPSU, the Komsomol prepared young people aged fourteen to twenty-eight for Party membership. Children aged nine to fourteen joined the Pioneer wing, while politically mature children below the age of nine joined the Little Octobrists. By the 1970s and 1980s membership had reached the forty million mark.

66

International Diplomacy

Diplomacy in some form has been oiling the waters of relations between clans, cities and kingdoms since people first recognised the value of getting along with their neighbours instead of attacking them. In Europe, the roots of modern diplomacy are frequently traced back to the early Renaissance and the city states of northern Italy. By the seventeenth century, French had replaced Latin as the *lingua franca* of diplomacy, and although itself now largely replaced by English, the influence of French is still much in evidence in many of the terms used. At the Congress of Vienna in 1815, when parts of Europe were 'reorganised' after the Napoleonic Wars, four senior diplomatic ranks were recognised:

- Ambassadors, legates and nuncios

- Envoys and ministers

- Ministers resident

- Chargés d'affaires

But in 1961 after the Vienna Convention on Diplomatic Relations, the rank of Ministers resident (a diplomatic agent resident at a foreign government) was dropped, leaving three ranks of head of mission (principal official of a diplomatic mission), in descending order:

DIPLOMATIC OFFICIALS

Ambassadors or nuncios (papal ambassadors)
Accredited to the host country's head of state and other heads of mission of equivalent rank.

Envoys extraordinary, ministers plenipotentiary (with 'full powers'), and internuncios (papal envoys) and other representatives
Accredited to the host country's head of state.

Chargés d'affaires *(ad hoc)*
Usually accredited to the host country's minister of foreign affairs, rather than to the head of state.

Chargés d'affaires *(ad interim)*
A diplomatic agent deputising for an absent head of mission.

DIPLOMATIC CORRESPONDENCE	The correspondence between one state and another is highly stylised, using elaborate established courtesy phrases. It takes the form of letters (e.g. letters of credence granting diplomatic accreditation, letters of recall – of an ambassador) or notes. Some of the most commonly used are listed below in descending order of formality and importance. However, diplomacy is not immune to the recent rapid changes in communication technology, and many diplomats now also communicate by email, when they must use all their innate prudence and vigilance to guard against an over-impulsive click of the 'send' button.
First-person note	For the most important correspondence, such as between a head of mission and the head of a foreign ministry or a foreign diplomatic mission. Signed.
Third-person note	Written in the third person, so the first and second person pronouns (I, we, you, your) must not be used. With a few exceptions, not signed but initialled in the lower right corner of the last page. Third-person notes include:

Note verbale
As the name implies, a note verbale was originally a written record of information delivered orally. It begins with a courtesy phrase.

Memorandum
A written statement on any, usually routine, subject. Courtesy phrases are used if it is custom.

Aide-mémoire
An 'aid to memory', a note summarising the key points of an informal conversation or interview, without committing the issuing delegation's country to the contents. It does not begin with a courtesy phrase.

Bout de papier
A 'piece of paper', a very informal way of presenting written information.

Other notes	These include the **Note diplomatique**, a formal note between governments, with courtesy phrases; **Note collective**, addressed to or sent by two or more governments (little used due to the difficulty in getting all parties to agree on its wording); **Circular diplomatic note**, an identical note from a single state to multiple states.

67

The Sovereign's Bodyguard

On 22 August 1485, Henry Tudor defeated English king Richard III at the Battle of Bosworth Field, founded the Tudor dynasty as King Henry VII, and created the King's Body Guard of the Yeomen of the Guard. Not bad for a day's work!

The yeomen are instantly recognisable by their historic uniform – red and gold tunics with a striped cross belt worn from the left shoulder, white ruffled collars, scarlet stockings and black Tudor hats – the ensemble, complete with sword and halberd, weighs an exhausting 11 kg (24 lb) or so. The oldest military corps in existence in Britain, today they form the sovereign's ceremonial bodyguard and are all former officers and sergeants of the British armed services.

Captain
Traditionally a peer of the realm, he sometimes holds another position in the Royal Household (see page 113).

Lieutenant
The holder of this position, created in 1669, must have served within the Army or the Marines and attained a rank of at least major.

Clerk of the Cheque
Not, as might be expected from the name, the treasurer, but rather the Guard's adjutant and secretary.

Ensign
The standard-bearer. Originally above the Clerk of the Cheque in the hierarchy, but in 1927 King George V declared that the latter had greater authority and reversed the positions. The office was created in 1668 and still exists, although it appears that the standard itself was destroyed in a fire in St James's Palace in 1809.

Exon
The most junior officer is so named because these officers were exempt from normal duties – the name is thought to derive from the pronunciation of the French word 'exempt'.

Non-commissioned ranks

Other ceremonial bodyguards
These include two curiously named positions dating from Tudor times

Messenger Sergeant Major
Responsible for the day-to-day management of the Yeomen, the MSM is also the Wardrobe Keeper.

Yeoman Bed Goer and Yeoman Bed Hanger
These titles still exist, although the post holders are no longer required to make the sovereign's bed.

Gold Stick
This office is shared by the Colonels of the Life Guards and the Blues and Royals army regiments. When one Gold Stick is on duty, the other is known as Gold-Stick-in-Waiting. The office is named for the gilt-headed rod they carry.

Silver Stick
This office is held by the Commander of the Household Cavalry. Silver-Stick-in-Waiting is deputy to Gold-Stick-in-Waiting, obviously.

A ROYAL VIGIL
In April 2002, the Yeomen of the Guard took part in the round-the-clock silent vigil at the lying-in-state of Queen Elizabeth the Queen Mother in London's Westminster Hall.

The Yeomen Warders (aka Beefeaters) who guard the Tower of London are a detachment of the Yeomen of the Guard. Today, their role is to entertain visitors with tales of the Tower's famous captives, many of whom met an unfortunate end there.

68

The King's Musketeers

Founded in 1622 by Louis XIII, the two companies of the Mousquetaires du Roi served the French monarch until 1815, although they were disbanded and reinstated several times during that period. They formed part of the royal household and were the king's guard when he was away from his royal residences. Membership was in principle reserved for members of the aristocracy, and each musketeer would have his own servant(s).

In the early days, the musketeers wore the famous blue cassock over their own clothes, but a full uniform evolved over time. From 1665, the 1st Company rode white or light grey horse, earning them the nickname *mousquetaires gris* (grey musketeers), and the 2nd company black, the *mousquetaires noirs* (black musketeers). The ranks varied over the years but were broadly as follows:

Capitaine (Captain)
This rank was officially taken by the king.

Capitaine-Lieutenant (Captain-Lieutenant)

Lieutenant

Sous-Lieutenant (Sub-Lieutenant)

Enseigne (Ensign)

Cornette (Cornet)
The most junior officer rank.

Maréchal des Logis
A senior NCO, the equivalent of a warrant officer.

Brigadier
A senior NCO, the equivalent of a sergeant-major.

Sous-Brigadier
A sergeant.

Fourier
Quartermaster-Sergeant.

Mousquetaire
Soldier, originally armed with a matchlock musket *(mousquet)*.

SWASHBUCKLER SUPREME: FACT OR FICTION

D'Artagnan, the most famous musketeer of them all, who featured in Alexandre Dumas' The Three Musketeers, was based on veteran musketeer Gatien de Courtilz de Sandras' fictionalised account of the life of Charles de Batz de Castelmore d'Artagnan, a 'real' musketeer who served under Louis XIV. D'Artagnan was indeed a brave soldier who rose to the rank of Capitaine-Lieutenant, although it is not clear just how many of the fictional d'Artagnan's flamboyant exploits are rooted in truth.

69

The British Royal Household

Since 1688, Britain has had a constitutional monarchy, whereby Parliament, not the sovereign, is the ruling power; virtually all countries with a monarchy now have the same system. However, with numerous State and public duties to perform, being king or queen is still a very demanding role, requiring a large support network. In Britain, each member of the royal family has its own household. The sovereign's household currently has three Great Officers – the Lord Chamberlain, who coordinates the five main departments that keep the royal machine running smoothly, and the Lord Steward and the Master of the Horse, whose roles are ceremonial.

The Private Secretary's Office
This department supports the sovereign's work as Head of State. The team's responsibilities include organising official visits, both at home and abroad, and advising on constitutional matters.

The Privy Purse and Treasurer's Office
Besides managing the royal finances, it covers practical aspects of running the family 'firm', such as human resources and technology.

The Master of the Household's Department
Masterminds both official and private entertaining and includes all those involved in hospitality, such as caterers and florists.

The Lord Chamberlain's Office
Manages all the ceremonial events, from State visits and the State Opening of Parliament to royal weddings and garden parties, and is also responsible for travel.

Royal Collection
Manages the care and presentation of the royal art collection, as well as the opening of the official royal residences to the public.

Specialist households

These include the ecclesiastical household, which includes clergy and organist/choirmaster/composer for the Chapels Royal, and the medical household, which covers every eventuality from surgery to dentistry. The Queen has separate Royal Households in Scotland and Canada.

Among the more unusual positions are:

The Queen's Piper

The sovereign has awakened each morning to the sound of bagpipes since Queen Victoria appointed the first piper in 1843. Queen Elizabeth the Queen Mother also had a piper, whose duty was to play at her request.

Marker of the Swans

All mute swans in open water in Britain are officially owned by the sovereign, and the holder of this post, established in the twelfth century, organises the annual 'swan upping', when unmarked birds are ringed.

Official Harpist to the Prince of Wales

The harp is the national instrument of Wales. The post of Official Harpist lapsed during the reign of Queen Victoria but was revived in 2000 by Prince Charles, the current Prince of Wales.

LOYAL TO THE ROYALS

Each year at Christmas, the sovereign presents every member of the Royal Household with a traditional Christmas pudding and a gift. The value of the gift is determined by length of service.

Upper- and middle-class Victorian households were run like small businesses, staffed according to size, location and the family income. Even modest households would have at least a maid-of-all-work. Reflecting upstairs society as a whole, a strict hierarchy operated downstairs.

MAIN HOUSEHOLD STAFF

FIRST LEVEL
Butler
Head of the male staff; in charge of the wine cellar, supervising family dining and social events, employing and supervising footmen and other male staff. In larger households, he was supported by an Under Butler.

Housekeeper
Head of the female staff; in charge of running the household, cleaning, maintenance, household accounts, liaison with tradesmen and supervising the maids' work.

SECOND LEVEL
Valet (aka *Groom of the Chamber*)
Attended to all personal needs of the master of the house, preparing his clothes, helping him to wash, shave and dress.

Lady's Maid
Attended to all the needs of the mistress and her wardrobe, including hairdressing.

THIRD LEVEL
Footman
Responsible for the footwear, polishing the silver, answering the door and assisting the butler. Large households would include a First Footman, a Lady's Footman and a number of Under Footmen. Footmen were usually required to be fit specimens of manhood who looked good in a uniform, to add style to a household.

Housemaids
Responsible for cleaning all the rooms, preparing and lighting fires, changing bedlinen and emptying the chamber pots. Chamber Maids were responsible for the bedrooms and Parlour Maids for the living and reception rooms. In larger households there would be Under Housemaids or a Second and Third Housemaid.

Laundry Maid

Responsible for washing and cleaning the family's clothes and bedlinen. Laundry Maids might live out and come in as and when required.

WOMEN'S WORK

According to the census of 1851, domestic service of all kinds was the single biggest area of employment for women (40 per cent of females in provincial cities and rising to 50 per cent in London).

SUB DEPARTMENTS

THE KITCHEN

Although the Housekeeper and Butler had seniority in the kitchen, in practice it was the province of the Cook. The quality of the Cook could make or break a household's social standing.

Cook

Responsible for cooking meals for the family, guests and servants, supervising kitchen staff and planning menus (with the Butler and Housekeeper).

Kitchen Maid

Assistant to the Cook, responsible for the cleanliness of the kitchen and food preparation; large households could maintain several kitchen maids.

Scullery Maid

The scullery was a small room at the back of the kitchen used for washing up. The Scullery Maid was a kitchen dogsbody, subordinate to the kitchen maids, responsible for washing up and cleaning pots.

Houseboy

A boy who waited on the other servants.

THE NURSERY

Households with children maintained nursery staff.

Head Nurse/Nanny

In charge of the family's babies and children until the girls were old enough for a governess and the boys were sent away to school. A large family would require Under Nurses as well.

Nursery Maid
Responsible for cleaning the nursery, washing nappies, and so on.

OUTSIDE STAFF

Coachman
Responsible for the overall functioning of the stables and the driving and maintenance of the family coach. A large household could also have had an Under Coachman.

Groom
Responsible for grooming the horses.

Stable Boy
Subject to orders from the Groom and Coachman, responsible for mucking out the stables.

Head Gardener
Responsible for the grounds, garden and greenhouses; planning and planting flowers and vegetables; providing cut flowers for the house and produce for the kitchen.

Under Gardener
Under orders from the Head Gardener.

Labourers
Employed on ad hoc basis for heavy work in the garden.

NEITHER FISH NOR FOWL
Governesses, employed to educate the girls of the family, occupied an ambiguous social position; they were not considered actual servants, as they were often the poorer members of middle-class families.

Honours and Awards

The UK honours system recognises those who have made achievements in public life and committed themselves to serving their country and community, improving the lives of others and being outstanding in their own fields. It is overseen by the Cabinet Office Honours and Appointments Secretariat and submitted to the Queen through the prime minister. Civilian gallantry awards are given to those who have demonstrated bravery attempting to save or saving the life of a British citizen who isn't a family member or friend.

Companion of Honour
Founded by George V in 1917 and awarded to those who have made a major contribution to the arts, science, medicine or government over a long period of time. There are sixty-five members at any one time. The order bears the motto 'In action faithful and in honour clear'.

Knight/Dame
Awarded for major contributions in any activity, usually at national level. It harks back to the days of medieval chivalry as does the manner in which it is bestowed: the accolade or touch of a sword by the sovereign. Women do not receive the accolade and are addressed as 'Dame'.

Commander of the Order of the British Empire (CBE)
This is awarded for having a prominent but lesser role at national level, or a leading role at regional level. You can also be given a CBE for a distinguished, innovative contribution to any area.

Officer of the Order of the British Empire (OBE)
This is awarded for having a major role locally in any activity, including people whose work has made them known nationally in their chosen area.

Member of the Order of the British Empire (MBE)
Awarded for an outstanding achievement or service to the community, which will have had a long-term, significant impact and stand out as an example to others.

British Empire Medal (BEM)
Awarded for a 'hands-on' service to the local community. This could be a long-term charitable or voluntary activity, or innovative work of a relatively short duration (three to four years) that has made a significant difference.

Overseas Territories Police and Fire Service Medals
Given for service in British Overseas Territories.

Royal Victorian Order (RVO)
An award given by the Queen – usually to people who have helped her personally, like members of the Royal Household staff or British ambassadors.

The George Cross
First-level civilian medal for bravery: awarded for acts of heroism and courage in extreme danger.

The George Medal
Second-level civilian medal for bravery: awarded for acts of great bravery.

The Queen's Gallantry Medal
Third-level civilian medal for bravery: awarded for inspiring acts of bravery.

The Queen's Commendation for Bravery
The Queen's Commendation for Bravery in the Air
For risk to life.

Twice a year – at New Year and on the Queen's official birthday in June – *The Gazette* publishes a list of recipients of what is sometimes referred to colloquially as a 'gong' – an honorary award for exceptional achievement or service in the UK or any of the Commonwealth countries, listed below in descending order of importance. With the exception of the most ancient orders, whose members are chosen by the sovereign, nominations for the awards are made either by government departments or by members of the public.

The Most Noble Order of the Garter

The oldest order of chivalry, inspired by tales of King Arthur's Knights of the Round Table and originally for male aristocrats only. Members are styled Knight or Lady of the Garter.

Founded by/date: Edward III/1348

Who: Men and women

Why: Recognition of public service

Number of members: Twenty-four knights + members of royal family

Motto: *Honi soit qui mal y pense* ('Shame on him who thinks this evil')

Designatory letters: KG/LG

The Most Ancient and Most Noble Order of the Thistle

The origins of this Scottish order of knighthood are unclear, but it may have been founded in the fifteenth century by James III of Scotland, who adopted the thistle as the royal plant. The order was revived in 1687 by James VII of Scotland (James II of England), lapsed when he was deposed, and was revived again by Queen Anne in 1703. Members are styled Knight or Lady of the Thistle.

Founded by/date: James III/fifteenth century

Who: Scottish men and women

Why: Significant contribution to national life

Number of members: Sixteen + members of royal family

Motto: *Nemo me impune lacessit* ('No one provokes me with impunity')

Designatory letters: KT/LT

The Most Honourable Order of the Bath

The curious name derives from the purification ritual of bathing that once formed part of the knighthood ceremony. There are three grades (see below).

Founded by/date: George I/1725

Who: Men and women

Why: Military service or exemplary civilian merit

Grades (number of members): Knight/Dame Grand Cross (120), Knight/Dame Commander (355), Companion (1,925)

Motto: *Tria juncta in uno* ('Three joined in one')

Designatory letters:
Knight/Dame Grand Cross – GCB
Knight/Dame Commander – KCB/DCB
Companion – CB

KNIGHTS BACHELOR
A 'men only' knighthood, not attached to any particular order of chivalry. This most ancient but also most lowly knightly honour is often awarded to those in the world of sport or entertainment. Knights Bachelor are styled 'Sir' but have no designatory letters.

The Order of Merit

Comparable to the French Legion d'Honneur and the American Congressional Gold Medal. Although there is no knighthood attached to the honour, its exclusivity and prestigious reputation make it highly desirable.

Founded by/date: Edward VII/1902

Who: Men and women

Why: Exceptional distinction in the armed forces or the fields of arts, sciences and learning

Number of members: Twenty-four

Motto: For merit

Designatory letters: OM

Companion of Honour

A sort of 'junior' Order of Merit, this award was created to recognise services of national importance.

Founded by/date: George V/1917

Who: Men and women

Why: Contribution to the arts, science, medicine or government over a long period

Number of members: Sixty-five

Motto: In action faithful and in honour clear

Designatory letters: CH

The Most Distinguished Order of St Michael and St George

Founded to recognise distinguished citizens of the Ionian Islands (now part of Greece, but at that time under British protection) and Malta. There are three grades (listed below).

Founded by/date: Prince Regent/1818

Who: Men and women

Why: Service in a foreign country or in relation to foreign or Commonwealth affairs

Grades (number of members): Knight/Dame Grand Cross (125), Knight/Dame Commander (375), Companion (1,750)

Motto: *Auspicium melioris aevi* ('Token of a better age')

Designatory letters:
Knight/Dame Grand Cross – GCMG
Knight/Dames Commander – KCMG/DCMG
Companions – CMG

Royal Victorian Order

Instituted by Queen Victoria in 1896, it rewards personal services rendered to the monarch. There are five grades (listed below).

Founded by/date: Queen Victoria/1896

Who: Men and women

Why: Personal services rendered to the monarch

Number of members: Unlimited

Grades: Knight/Dame Grand Cross, Knight/Dame Commander, Commander, Lieutenant, Member

Motto: Victoria

Designatory letters:
Knight/Dame Grand Cross – GCVO
Knight/Dames Commander – KCVO/DCVO
Commander – CVO
Lieutenant – LVO
Member – MVO

The Most Excellent Order of the British Empire

Founded to recognise ordinary people who rendered service to the nation, both military and civilian, originally during World War I. The majority of people receiving a 'gong' will be admitted to one of the five grades (see below), of which the two highest are knighthoods.

Founded by/date: George V/1917

Who: Men and women

Why: Exceptional achievement or service

Number of members: Unlimited

Grades: Knight/Dame Grand Cross, Knight/Dame Commander, Commander, Officer, Member

Motto: For God and the Empire

Designatory letters:
Knight/Dame Grand Cross – GBE
Knight/Dame Commander – KBE/DBE
Commander – CBE
Officer – OBE
Member – MBE

FORM AN ORDERLY LINE
Since the Middle Ages, knighthood has been conferred in a ritual act known as 'the accolade'. In the UK, this takes the form of the sovereign (or delegate) dubbing the kneeling recipient on both shoulders with a sword – Queen Elizabeth II uses the sword that belonged to her father, George VI. Neither women receiving a damehood nor clergy receiving a knighthood are dubbed.

On 15 June 1574, Elizabeth I reinforced the sumptuary laws (Enforcing Statutes of Apparel) laid down by her father Henry VIII. Concerned that profligate spending on the latest ruff would lead to 'the manifest decay of the whole realm' along with 'the wasting and undoing of a great number of young gentlemen', the strict laws also ensured that everyone who was anyone knew their place. They specified the colour, material and type of clothing each individual could wear, acting as a kind of sixteenth-century soccer strip, ensuring the onlooker could identify others as 'one of us' – signalling their rank and privilege at a glance. Transgressions were rewarded with harsh punishment, via fines and loss of property or title, although to begin with the queen in her 'princely clemency' was content simply to 'give warning to her loving subjects to reform themselves'.

Extracts from these precise and lengthy laws:

Purple silk, 'cloth of gold tissued', sable fur
Only to be worn by the king and queen and certain of their immediate family (including the king's mother). Permissible for dukes, marquises and earls but only in certain garments (doublets, jerkins, cloak linings, gowns, hose); Knights of the Garter could wear purple in mantles only.

Cloth of gold, silver, tinseled satin, silk, cloth mixed or embroidered with any gold or silver
For viscounts and above only, also barons and 'other persons of like degree' provided it was in doublets, jerkins, cloak linings, gowns and hose.

Woollen cloth 'made out of the realm' (i.e. imported) in caps only; crimson or scarlet velvet; certain black furs; embroidery or tailor's work involving gold or silver or pearls
Limited to dukes, marquises, earls and their children, viscounts, barons, and 'knights being companions of the Garter, or any person being of the Privy Council'.

The laws also extended to hardware

'Gilt, silvered or damasked' spurs, swords, rapiers, daggers, certain knives, buckles or girdles, gilt
Only to be sported by knights and barons' sons, and above, and also by 'gentlemen in ordinary office attendant upon the Queen's majesty's person' ... providing they left their spurs at home.

Dressing Up and Down

On any occasion where dress code is specified, it's male attire that drives the choice of outfit. The rules on colour, style and accessories are often rigid, while women are given vague guidelines but left to create their own sartorial triumphs – or disasters. Here's how the hierarchy works, from the smartest to the (relatively) scruffiest.

White tie

The strictest, very definitely the starchiest, but ultimately the least likely to be required, although until World War II white tie was evening dress *de rigueur* for gentlemen. With the exception of the black dress trousers, tailcoat, shoes (and of course socks), everything is white: dress shirt (including studs and cufflinks), detachable wing collar, bow tie, waistcoat. Women attending a white tie occasion are required to wear full-length, formal evening dress, traditionally with long white gloves. Married women may wear a tiara, and all women can go to town with jewellery.

Black tie

Still formal, still a bit starchy, and still in regular use for evening events. Black is the predominant colour – for the dinner jacket (*aka* a DJ, or tuxedo), trousers, shoes, socks, shirt studs, and of course the bow tie, which English etiquette guide Debrett's advises should be 'proportionate to the size of the wearer'. Only the evening shirt is white, with a turn-down collar, and *please* – no ruffles. Women have far more choice here (and therefore far more scope to get it wrong!) – a long evening dress or skirt, or a knee-length cocktail dress, or even wide-legged trousers worn with a flowing top.

Morning dress

Formal day dress, as the name suggests – it is never worn at events starting after six o'clock in the evening. A black or grey morning coat is worn with grey or grey-and-black striped trousers, a white or pale-coloured shirt, and a waistcoat – all the buttons done up if double-breasted, or with the lowest button undone if single-breasted. A tie rather than a cravat, and the top hat is only worn at the races; otherwise, it's carried. Women wear something smart and modest – a dress or skirt with a tailored jacket, daytime jewellery such as pearls, and to complete the outfit – depending on the occasion – a hat.

Lounge suits

Despite the rather smart description, just a general-purpose suit and tie, which are worn for business and slightly formal social events. The style of suit is down to the wearer's preference – three-piece, which includes a waistcoat, or two-piece, without a waistcoat. And standards must still be observed – the shirt must be worn with a tie, and the top button must be done up. Women wear a toned-down version of their morning dress outfit.

Smart casual

Not as simple as it sounds, not only because there's far more choice but also because there's formal smart casual and informal smart casual. 'Formal' means smart separates with a casual shirt rather than a suit, and definitely no jeans; 'informal' means the same, but smart jeans are permitted, and a polo shirt. T-shirts and trainers do not constitute smart casual. The same applies to women, who should avoid anything resembling business wear but also shun sportswear and trainers. Debrett's advice is: if in doubt, ask your host or hostess for guidance.

To the modern eye, the UK's traditional court dress of flowing robes and white horsehair wigs looks quaint, antiquated and eccentric. Of course, when wigs were added to the legal dress code in the eighteenth century, everyone in polite society was wearing one, men and women alike. But today? Not so much...

However, the court service has recently updated its image – barristers now only wear the wig and gown to lend gravitas in criminal cases and even judges are toning down. Heads of Division (listed below) and Court of Appeal judges wear a court coat and waistcoat with trousers or a skirt, 'bands' (two strips of fabric hanging from a collar), a black silk gown and a short wig for criminal cases, while for civil cases they don a simple 'civil robe', introduced in 2008, with bands of various colours to denote seniority, and no wig.

HEADS OF DIVISION

Lord Chief Justice
Head of the Judiciary in England and Wales, President of the Courts of England and Wales and Head of Criminal Justice.

Master of the Rolls
So-called because originally the post-holder was responsible for the safe-keeping of documents of national importance, written on parchment rolls. The Master of the Rolls is a judge of the Court of Appeal and President of its Civil Division.

President of the Queen's Bench Division
The largest of the UK's three High Court Divisions, it has the most varied jurisdiction, ranging from civil cases, including crime, to specialist areas such as the Admiralty Court, which handles shipping and maritime disputes.

President of the Family Division
As the name suggests, it deals with family matters, including divorce and adoption. Judges hearing family cases in Chambers wear a suit, deemed less intimidating than even the civil robe.

Chancellor of the High Court
The holder of this post is president of the Chancery Division of the High Court, which deals with disputes involving property. The Chancellor wears the new civil robe in court, but sports a gold robe on ceremonial occasions.

SUPREME COURT

Supreme Court Judges

Judges at the Supreme Court (set up in 2009 to replace the Law Lords) generally wear conventional business clothing, although on ceremonial occasions don a black damask robe with generous amounts of gold decoration. In 2011, it was announced that lawyers appearing at the Supreme Court would also have the option to dispense with court dress, subject to agreement.

COURT OF APPEAL

Lord Justices of Appeal

The Court of Appeal has a Civil and a Criminal Division and is the final court of appeal for the majority of cases. Like the Heads of Division, they are referred to as Lord/Lady Justice [Surname]. Dress is as described in the introduction.

HIGH COURT

High Court Judges

These try serious criminal cases and important civil cases. If they're dealing with criminal cases, they wear red robes, earning them the title 'red judges', and for civil cases they wear the new civil robe with red tabs at the neck. But on 'red-letter days', such as the sovereign's birthday, all High Court judges don the red robe.

A CHANGE OF COLOUR

In Scotland, High Court judges wear a white robe embellished with bold red crosses, while Court of Session judges wear a crimson robe with darker red crosses.

BOW DOWN TO THE CROWN

Those entering or leaving a courtroom in England or Wales are required to bow respectfully towards the judge or magistrate who is presiding. However, the bow is actually directed at the Royal Coat of Arms behind the bench, as a mark of recognition that justice stems from the Crown.

The UK Judiciary

Her Majesty's Courts & Tribunals Service (HMCTS) applies to England, Wales and Northern Ireland; Scotland has its own judiciary. At its head is the Supreme Court (UKSC), whose twelve justices hear appeals on arguable points of law of the 'greatest public importance'. In January 2017 they ruled on a landmark case – the most important in the UK's recent history – declaring that an Act of Parliament was required to trigger Article 50 to begin the process of leaving the European Union. The ruling did not apply to the Scottish Parliament or the Welsh or Northern Ireland assemblies.

Supreme Court
The final court of appeal for all UK civil cases (including Scotland) and for criminal cases from England, Wales and Northern Ireland.

Court of Appeal
In two divisions: the Criminal Division, which hears appeals from the Crown Court, and the Civil Division, which hears appeals from the High Court, tribunals and certain cases from county courts.

High Court
Includes the Queen's Bench Division, the Administrative Court, the Family Division, the Divisional Court, the Chancery Division and the Divisional Court.

Crown Court
For trials of indictable offences, appeals from magistrates' courts and cases for sentence.

Magistrates' Court
For trials of summary offences (can be heard by a magistrate alone, rather than judge and jury), committals to the Crown Court, family proceedings courts and youth courts.

County Courts
For the majority of civil litigation.

Tribunals
For appeals on matters such as immigration, social security and tax.

Prison Pecking Order

Although the crime committed plays a part, the pecking order in prison is mostly governed by inmates' sheer physical strength and/or access to drugs, tobacco and money. The more vulnerable keep their heads down or resort to supplying others with sex or, if they have the means, chocolate, tobacco, drugs, toiletries and so on. In return they receive protection. Those identified as vulnerable because of their general inability to cope with prison are placed 'on protection' for their own good by the staff. Others 'on protection' may include paedophiles and those guilty of sexual crimes.

In England and Wales, male inmates are categorised as A, B, C or D and once sentenced are sent to a prison with the appropriate structure in place for their category. The pecking order described above can be found in all categories of prison.

Category A
Those who pose the most threat to the public, the police or national security should they escape. Offences include murder, rape, terrorism and crimes involving class A drugs. The prisons are designed to make escape impossible.

Category B
Inmates do not need to be held in the highest-security conditions but escape is still made very difficult. They may have committed a serious crime before, or have served/be serving a previous sentence of ten years or more.

Category C
Offenders cannot be trusted in an open prison but are unlikely to make any real attempt to escape. They may have served a sentence of twelve months or more for offences including violence, arson, sex offences and drug dealing.

Category D
Inmates can be trusted to wander around the prison grounds unescorted or to work in the community. It applies to those who fit into none of the above categories, and non-violent offenders, e.g. fraudsters, who pose a low risk to the public.

Top Marks for Education

The rankings of the best education systems in the world are published every year but vary depending on the organisation conducting the survey and the criteria being taken into account, as do the systems themselves. However, some countries feature in the top ten more frequently than others.

SOUTH KOREA

Education here is seen as a driver of social mobility as well as a path to a good career and the teaching profession is well respected. Students are highly motivated but pressurised. With a literacy rate of around 98 per cent, the majority of students complete high school but competition for places at university is fierce. Many children attend *hagwon*, fee-paying after-hours crammers, some as young as kindergarten age, and some children attend school seven days a week.

PRESCHOOL
Kindergarten (optional, usually fee-paying) 3–6 years.

PRIMARY
Elementary school (compulsory, free of charge)
6–12/13 years.
Subjects include English, fine arts, science, moral education, music.

SECONDARY
Middle school (compulsory, free of charge) 12/13–15/16 years.
Teachers specialise in core subjects. Optional subjects include ethics, home economics, history. Discipline is strict.

High school (state-owned or fee-paying) 16–18 years.
Some schools specialise, others have a more general curriculum.

OR

Vocational high school or college (state-owned or fee-paying) 16–18 years.
Subjects include agriculture, technology, commerce.

TERTIARY EDUCATION

Colleges and universities Nearly 90 per cent of students move on to higher education but only 40 per cent complete it – it is mostly fee-paying.

Degrees: bachelor's (four years), master's (two years), doctorate (three years).

EXAM CONDITIONS

The local community does its best to help students taking the all-important entrance exam for the elite colleges that can be a passport to a good career and even marriage. Businesses open one hour later than usual to ensure the roads are clear for students to arrive on time, and airport landings and take-offs are halted for the thirty-minute duration of language listening tests.

Finland's unorthodox education system is among the best in the world and Finland frequently tops the rankings. Education is free at all levels, apart from adult education. The government decides what should be taught but not how. There are no league tables and no school inspections, and only one set of matriculation exams at age sixteen.

Early childhood education and care (ECEC)
Preschool education at daycare centres and clubs, 0–5 years, optional.

Pre-primary
6 years old, compulsory.

Comprehensive school
7–16 years, compulsory. Classes in the last three years of attendance are run by subject-specialist teachers. Comprehensive school ends with a set of four compulsory tests – one is the mother tongue (usually Finnish; Swedish is the second national language and Saami is also spoken), plus three other subjects as chosen by the student; they may also take optional extra tests.

General upper secondary school/vocational institutions
16–19 years, 90 per cent of children go on to this level. Vocational courses include at least six months of work experience.

University or polytechnic
The emphasis is on scientific research at the universities, with a more practical approach at polytechnics. Students may be required to sit entrance tests as there are more applicants than places available.
Degrees: bachelor's (three years), master's (two years), doctorate (six years).

Divide and Rule

There is an agreed 'order of operations' in mathematics, starting with the calculations inside brackets, and then descending via those involving indices (roots and square roots) and division and multiplication to the easier operations of addition and subtraction. The acronym BIDMAS helps you work out the order in which the law applies to different elements of a complicated operation. Let's take it from the top:

First do all the calculations in **B**rackets.

Then tackle the **I**ndices (powers such as squares, square roots).

Next do the **D**ivision and **M**ultiplication (start on the left and work them out in the order you find them).

And lastly, do the **A**ddition and **S**ubtraction (when only addition and subtraction are left, work them out in the order you find them, again starting from the left).

Therefore

$4 + 2 \times 4 = 24$ (wrong: do not add $4 + 2$ and then multiply $\times 4$)
$4 + 2 \times 4 = 12$ (correct: multiply 2×4 and then add 4)

$6 \times (5 + 3) = 33$ (wrong: do not multiply 6×5 and then add 3)
$6 \times (5 + 3) = 48$ (correct: do brackets first so 8×6)

Division and multiplication are regarded as being on the same level, which also applies to addition and subtraction – in both cases complete the calculations in the order of left to right:

$7 - 2 + 6 = 11$
$4 \div 2 \times 5 = 10$

MNEMONICS
BIDMAS is sometimes known as BODMAS (O = order, numbers involving square roots or powers). In the USA it is known as PEMDAS (Parentheses, Exponents, Multiplication, Division, Addition and Subtraction, or to commit to memory more whimsically, Please Excuse My Dear Aunt Sally or Please Enter Math Data As Shown).

Creditworthiness

Credit scores are awarded not just to individuals – most people only find out they have one when they are unexpectedly turned down for a loan – but also to companies and countries. Several credit ratings agencies (Standard & Poor's, Fitch Ratings and Moody's) cover some 95 per cent of the ratings market between them. They award a letter score to debt issued by a corporation or government on the basis of that particular institution's creditworthiness (how likely they are to repay a debt) and vulnerability (how likely they are to default); higher grades indicate lower chances of default.

There is a range of systems for short-term debt, but for long-term lending, a typical rating would range from AAA–D (with lower-case letters and +/- signs sometimes added for fine-tuning, as detailed below).

Prime
AAA (an extremely good capacity for repayment)

High-grade
AA+, AA, AA– (a very strong capacity)

Upper medium grade
A+, A, A– (a strong capacity)

Lower medium grade
BBB+, BBB, BBB– (an adequate capacity)

Non-investment grade (speculative)
BB+, BB, BB– (vulnerable, and open to default)

Highly speculative
B+, B, B– (vulnerable and more likely to default)

Involving substantial risk
CCC+, CCC, CCC– (currently vulnerable)

Extremely speculative
CC (currently highly vulnerable)

At risk of imminent default
C (currently highly vulnerable, default likely)

In default
DDD, DD, D (the debtor has failed to pay an obligation)

FROM A TO D
These ratings are extremely important in determining how much interest countries have to offer on the debt they issue – essentially, it is an indicator of how much they have to pay to access credit markets. But no country is immune to the ignominy of having their rating downgraded. Political and economic upheaval mean that even normally stable countries can be stripped of their triple A ratings by one or other of the agencies, as has happened to the UK, USA, Finland and France.

The eBay Star System

Feedback stars on the online auction and trading company eBay launched by Pierre Omidyar in 1995 appear next to a member's user ID and are awarded based on feedback. The higher the score, the more positive ratings a member has been awarded.

Star colour	Rating
Yellow	10 to 49
Blue	50 to 99
Turquoise	100 to 499
Purple	500 to 999
Red	1,000 to 4,999
Green	5,000 to 9,999
Yellow shooting star	10,000 to 24,999
Turquoise shooting star	25,000 to 49,999
Purple shooting star	50,000 to 99,999
Red shooting star	100,000 to 499,999
Green shooting star	500,000 to 999,999
Silver shooting star	1,000,000 or more

Marketing Effects

In 1961 Robert J. Lavidge and Gary A. Steiner devised this hierarchy designed to assist the era's Mad Men in guiding consumers through the various stages of purchasing to clinch that all-important deal, whether it be a bar of chocolate or a premium marque luxury car. This 'management speak' hierarchy is still in use today.

COGNITIVE STAGE

The consumer becomes aware of and gathers knowledge about a product.

Awareness
Making consumers aware of your brand/product. A 'no-brainer'; consumers must be aware that your product exists in order to buy it.

Knowledge
Ensuring information about your product and how it can be of value to the consumer is 'out there' and readily available.

AFFECTIVE STAGE

Emotions start to play a part and the consumer begins (hopefully) to find themselves drawn to your product/brand.

Liking
Building a liking for the product with consumers. Making sure any possible reservations are firmly dealt with by the marketing.

Preference
The consumer likes your product (good) but is now considering it alongside others (introducing an element of risk), evaluating their advantages and disadvantages. Now is the time to emphasise your product's unique selling points.

CONATIVE STAGE   After weighing up the pros and cons the consumer takes action and reaches for their wallet.

Conviction

The consumer is about to make a decision; any doubt about opting for your product in the (possibly wavering) consumer's mind must be quashed. Hand out free samples, discount vouchers . . . something to help the consumer decide and remain faithful to your product post-purchase rather than switch flightily to the next brand that offers a special deal.

Purchase

Make this easy (multiple paying options) and enjoyable (ensure the product is available and attractively displayed, special offers to make the consumer feel good . . .). Make it a pleasurable experience for the consumer and they may come back for more. Hooked. Job done!

Maslow's Hierarchy of Needs

A well-known system developed by American humanistic psychologist Abraham Maslow and first published in 1943, it ranks our fundamental motivations, from the basics needed to survive. The first four are described as deficiency needs and the fifth (self-actualisation) as a growth need. Once one level is satisfied, the desire to move on to the next kicks in. Managers use the hierarchy as a motivational tool, to identify and fulfil the needs of their staff.

ORIGINAL

1 Physiological
Air, food and drink, sleep, sex, warmth.

2 Safety
Security and freedom from fear.

3 Social needs
A sense of belonging and love, friendship and company.

4 Esteem
Social recognition and prestige, respect from others, personal worth.

5 Self-actualisation
Achieving one's full potential, including creatively.

EXTENDED

In the alternative-culture-led 1960s and 1970s, three more stages were slotted into the order:

4 (a) Cognitive – knowledge and understanding, curiosity, exploration, meaning.

4 (b) Aesthetic – appreciation and search for beauty, balance, etc.

6 Transcendence – helping others to achieve self-actualisation.

MILLENNIUM UPDATE
Some people might add 'Internet connection' to the list ...

Hazard Control

A 'health and safety' system devised to deal with potential hazards in industry and the workplace, minimising or ideally removing exposure to hazards altogether.

Eliminate
Remove the cause of the risk completely by changing a work process. For example, use equipment to move heavy items rather than have workers move them manually.

Substitute
Replace a hazardous practice/item with a safe alternative. For example, replace a substance used in powder form (hazardous particles may be inhaled) with one in crystal or pellet form.

Engineer controls
Methods built into the design of a plant or working process to isolate people at risk from the hazard. For example, reduce noise levels with noise-dampening equipment.

Administrative controls
Limit workers' exposure to a hazard or change their behaviour. For example, rotating schedules to limit exposure to a hazard, installing warning signs to avoiding touching eyes, lips, nose with contaminated hands.

Personal protective equipment (PPE)
Such as gloves, ear defenders, hard-hats, high-vis. jackets to control the hazard. The least effective method and the last resort since protective equipment may fail (leak/break) without warning.

Nineteen Eighty-Four

George Orwell's prescient and gloomy view of the future was published in 1949 but remains relevant today. His dystopian society where citizens are watched, tortured if they dare to think differently, and brainwashed into 'right thinking' is a chilling portrait of a state accountable to none or run by a despotic ruler.

Big Brother
Head of the totalitarian superstate Oceania.

Inner Party (2 per cent of the population)
'The Party' is the ruling class that governs and makes policy decisions. Members join the Party by passing an exam – 'The Party is not concerned with perpetuating its blood but with perpetuating itself.'

They enjoy: certain privileges such as being able to turn off the 'telescreens' that watch them, have servants, and access to coffee and tea, and comfortable homes.

Outer Party

An educated class, they administrate and implement the Party's policies but have no say in making them. They live in inferior homes, eat inferior food and are under constant supervision. They are also encouraged to inform on any non-right thinking party members.

They have access to: Victory cigarettes and gin (rather than wine). They must abstain from sex other than to procreate.

Proles (85 per cent of the population)
The workers perform menial tasks and labour, and are kept uneducated, but are not watched as they are not deemed sufficiently worthy.

They are fed: entertainment ('prolefeed') such as films, trashy novels, sport and pornography to keep the unthinking masses happy.

Animal Farm

Orwell's satire on society in Russia following the 1917 revolution was published in 1945. It describes how the animals (the working class) rebel against the cruel and neglectful farmer (the Tsar) and his men, and drive them out. Once alone the pigs draw up the Seven Commandments of Animalism, including the premise that 'All animals are equal', and start out to make a just society. But eventually the pigs begin to emerge as the most intelligent and start to take over, with pig-in-chief Napoleon as leader.

Napoleon (Stalin)
A large male Berkshire pig and the supreme leader, before whom everyone has to bow.

All other pigs (Stalin's ministers)
Who do Napoleon's bidding.

The dogs (Russian secret police)
They maintain law and order, ostensibly for the whole farm, but in reality spend most of their time protecting and working for Napoleon.

All the other animals (the working class)
Despite their strength in numbers they must obey the leader and the system without question.

A dystopian novel by Margaret Atwood set in a near future in Cambridge, Massachusetts, now part of the Republic of Gilead, a totalitarian theocratic state. In response to an unspecified environmental crisis, the birth rate has dropped below zero; the state's goal is to seize control of reproduction, and therefore of women and their bodies. Society is divided along rigid caste lines, with all women subservient to men, but also split into castes themselves. This has the toxic effect of demolishing solidarity among them, denying empathy and encouraging the willingness of women to oppress other women.

The Handmaid's Tale won the Arthur C. Clarke Award for the best science fiction novel in 1987.

See table opposite
* The Colonies are areas outside the Republic of Gilead that are environmentally toxic. People sent there face certain, usually lingering, death.

NAME	ROLE	UNIFORM	BENEFITS	PUNISHMENT
Men				
Commanders of the Faithful	Ruling class; entitled to Wife, Handmaid, Marthas and Guardians.	Black.	Allowed to drive cars, read, dictate the law.	
Eyes of God	Secret police.	Usually in disguise.	To spy on everyone, including the elite.	
Angels	Soldiers.	Military uniform.	Allowed to marry.	
Guardians of the Faith	Routine police and guard work. Unsuitable for other work as stupid, old, disabled or very young.	Green uniforms.	Young Guardians could be promoted to Angels when old enough.	
Gender Traitors	Homosexuals or other untraditional orientations.			Hanged or sent to the Colonies*.
Women				
Aunts	Unmarried, infertile or older women trained to monitor and control other women, especially Handmaids and Jezebels.	Brown, with leather belts and armed with cattle prods.	Confers the highest status.	
Handmaids	Young fertile women forced to bear children for Commanders and their Wives.	Red habits, gloves and shoes, white bonnets with wings to hide their faces.	Better fed than others, but not allowed to wear make-up or socialise with men.	Sent to Colonies* if do not produce a child after three two-year tours of duty.
Marthas	Older or infertile women without the Aunt mentality. Domestic duties: cooking, cleaning, child minding.	Green overalls.		
Econowives	Wives of low status men. Have to perform all female rites: childbearing, domestic work and companionship.	Red, blue and green dress.		
Wives	Wives of high status men.	Blue dress.	High status.	No autonomy or function.
Unwomen	Women who refuse or are unsuited for other roles: the sterile, some widows, nuns, lesbians, feminists, dissidents.			Sent to the Colonies*.
Jezebels	Prostitutes and entertainers. Available only to Commanders and guests.	Dress as stereotypes: cheerleaders, 'sexy outfits'.	Allowed to wear make-up, drink and socialise with men.	Sterilised. Work in regulated brothels. Rigidly controlled by the Aunts. Sent to the Colonies* when no longer attractive.

88

The Cowboy Cattle Drive

Cattle drives in the American West became large affairs following the American Civil War and with the expansion of the cattle industry. Between the 1860s and late 1880s, American cowboys operated an effective hierarchy of roles to aid communication and discipline during a drive, on which there could be around two to three thousand head of cattle to move long distances between states. The division of labour was generally as follows:

Trail boss
Responsible for the safety of the herd, keeping cattle and humans fed and watered, handling the money and maintaining the peace. He would be paid around ninety dollars a month.

Chuck wagon cook
Cooking three meals a day from the back of a chuck wagon, involving setting up and dismantling the 'kitchen' three times a day with each new camp, was no easy feat. The cook was also responsible for the personal belongings of the cowboys. He drew the second highest pay on a drive, around sixty bucks a month, and was not a guy to cross.

Point man
Guided the direction of the herd on the trail. He also watched out for hazards such as rattle snakes, coyotes and thieves. The point man pocketed around thirty to forty dollars.

Swing
Kept the herd together and ensured the flanks were not threatened by coyotes or raiding parties. The swing would ride a third of the way back from the point man and was paid the same wage.

Flank
Rode at the back to make sure slower cattle kept up with the herd. He was paid as the point man.

Drag

Ensured that any slower cattle caught up with the herd and pushed the slower animals forward. A dusty, dirty and unpleasant job usually reserved for new cowboys. The wage was around the same as the point man.

Wrangler

The horse wrangler looked after all the horses, kept them fed and well, and drove the remuda (herd of remount horses) ahead of the cattle. He would help the cook gather firewood and gathered around twenty-five dollars a month for himself.

FROM VAQUERO TO BUCKAROO

The original cowboys were the Mexican vaqueros (from the Spanish word vaca, meaning cow). They worked on ranches in Texas and Mexico. The English word buckaroo is an Anglicisation of vaquero.

89

Oil Rigged Up

Crews on oil drilling rigs operate in twelve-hour shifts with specific tasks and responsibilities. A typical organisational structure for a drill or rig crew is as follows:

Rig manager
Supervisor of the entire operation, with responsibility for all personnel, financial, technical and performance aspects of a rig.

Driller/Rig operator
Second-in-command to the rig manager, responsible for maintaining safety, supervising the crews and trouble-shooting problems.

Derrickhand
Works up to 25 m (82 ft) above the rig floor on a platform or 'monkey board' attached to the rig's derrick (the mast that supports the drilling equipment), guiding tubing and instruments in and out of the well; he also operates the drilling-fluid or 'mud' system (the viscous drilling fluid used to carry rock chips to the surface).

Motorhand
Responsible for the maintenance and repair of engines and other machinery.

Roughneck/Roustabout
An entry-level position on a rig with responsibility for cleaning pipelines, assembling, maintaining and repairing the drilling equipment.

CLIMBING THE RIG LADDER
A 'company man' or consultant is the on-site representative of the exploration company. 'Tool pushers' work closely with the company man to ensure the rig has all the tools, equipment and supplies it needs. Company men usually start as roustabouts and work their way up.

Most countries' road systems evolved slowly over the centuries, at least until the arrival of the internal combustion engine. It was the proliferation of the motor car along with growing populations that forced countries to adapt and expand their road networks, often in an urgent and reactive rather than a planned and proactive way. Throw variations between regions and states into the mix and it is not surprising that the numbering and classifying of roads has become a bone of contention for those who like a little order in their lives.

UK ROADS

By the 1920s it had become clear that the roads in England, Scotland and Wales needed something to help motorists on a grand day out in their Model Ts choose the best routes, and a rudimentary system was put in place that evolved over the years. But by the 1960s, Britain's roads were busy dealing with the first explosion of motoring for the masses so the system was overhauled and the roads reclassified.

Strategic road network (SRN)
Principally trunk roads, which are defined as motorways and significant A roads. They are 'nationally significant roads' for the transportation of goods and services and the use of the general public.

Primary road network (PRN)
Roads that provide the best route between primary destinations or 'places of traffic importance', which include towns and cities but also major bridges and tunnels. Confusingly, it also includes the SRN.

Special road
Roads on which certain types of traffic are banned, such as motorways, and some dual carriageways (roads where the traffic flow is separated by a central reservation).

A roads (numbered, e.g. A16)
These provide good transport links within and between different areas. Usually straight and to the point.

B roads (numbered, e.g. B4043)
They feed traffic between A roads and smaller roads.

Classified unnumbered roads

Known as 'C' roads, unofficially. These are smaller roads still and not worthy of a number, although some do have them, also unofficially.

Unclassified

Local roads for local traffic – 60 per cent of UK roads. Unclassified and unnumbered, although they may be numbered by local authorities beginning 'D' or 'U', but the numbers should not appear on public signage.

ROAD NUMBERING

England, Scotland and Wales are divided into nine zones radiating out from London. The zone number is the first digit in the road number, e.g. the southwest zone is number 3, where major roads include the A38, A39, A303. However, the next two to four digits are allocated in a much more haphazard way and many column inches (print and digital) have been devoted to the system's eccentricities.

FRENCH ROADS

The French classification appears deceptively simple, but idiosyncrasies such as the custom of changing the number of D roads at departmental boundaries, and the renumbering of some N roads as D mean that for the foreigner, the French road network should be approached with a degree of caution. Travellers proud of their traditional map-reading skills are recommended to navigate by following destinations and to ignore the road numbers.

Autoroutes

Numbered motorways, beginning 'A'. Some autoroutes are also allocated a second 'E' number (e.g. A43/E70), this being the European route number of a road that straddles more than one country. Some also have names that sound particularly evocative thanks to the French language, such as the Autoroute du Soleil, and the Autoroute des Deux Mers, which connects the Atlantic Ocean with the Mediterranean Sea.

Routes nationales

Main trunk roads, including dual carriageways, these are the shortest routes between major cities and towns. Numbers begin 'N' (e.g. N195), sometimes 'RN'. Some sections have autoroute status. The system dates back to 1811 and Napoleon's fourteen imperial highways that all began from Paris. Numbers 1–17 still radiate out from the capital.

Routes départmentales
Numbered minor roads beginning 'D' (e.g. D858) or less frequently RD. They vary considerably in terms of size and traffic, from small and narrow to downgraded routes nationales where thundering trucks bear down on brave cyclists. 'Bis' indicates a less crowded route (e.g. D211 bis).

Routes communales
Usually single-track roads that are local. Numbered 'C' or 'R'.

AMERICAN ROADS The Lancaster Turnpike, completed in 1795, was the first road to be engineered and planned in the USA. It connected Lancaster, Pennsylvania, with Philadelphia. One hundred and fifty years later, in 1956, construction of the interstate highway system was finally authorised, named the Dwight D. Eisenhower National System of Interstate and Defense Highways after its presidential champion.

Interstate highways
State-to-state roads (limited access) that are numbered (e.g. I–48), and often divided by a median (central reservation). The major north–south routes have odd numbers and east–west routes even numbers. Interstates with three-digit numbers are bypasses, beltways (ring roads) or spurs off the main interstates.

US States highways
Important national trunk roads connecting regions not served by the interstate highways. Numbered (e.g. US32), they vary from two-lane roads to dual carriageways. Sometimes known as federal highways, they also follow the north–south/east–west odd/even numbers system.

State highways
These range from local back roads to major four-lane trunk roads, but most are two-lane highways. Also known as state routes. Each state/territory has its own system for numbering.

County roads

Secondary roads numbered according to the state's system. Known in some states (e.g. Texas) as farm or ranch roads. County roads vary greatly, from freeways and expressways to unpaved roads in remote areas.

Other roads

Freeways – usually a toll-free divided highway with limited access via ramps; they enable traffic to flow unhindered (no traffic lights, crossroads/intersections, etc.). Interstate highways are also freeways.

Expressway – a divided highway with limited access. Interstate, US and State highways can also be expressways.

Limited-access road – for high-speed traffic. Access is by ramp (slip road). There are no intersecting roads (other than those accessed by a ramp) and you can normally only enter and exit from the right.

Parkway – may be a scenic road or a good-standard toll road.

Turnpike – usually a toll road of a good standard (but may also be free).

Frontage road – minor roads for local traffic, such as accessing motels and malls, farmland.

Business routes – divert off major roads to a town's business district.

Scenic byway – any classification of road that offers fine views.

ULTIMATE ROAD TRIP

Although it runs from Santa Monica to Chicago, US 66, one of the most famous roads in the world, is not an interstate highway. Known as the Main Street of America in the 1930s, because it ran through so many small towns, some segments were superseded by newer roads when the interstate highways were built, and it was ultimately decommissioned in 1985. Despite this, many organisations and individuals have preserved portions of it and Route 66 can be ridden again, but now as an Historic Route.

The Tour de France

Tactics loom large in the Tour de France, the most prestigious of the major cycle road races. Each team of nine riders works to promote their leader's chances of winning. The other eight riders take it in turns to take the energy-sapping hit of being exposed to wind resistance at the front. Those behind ride in the slipstream, conserving energy. Small groups of three to six near the front may attack by accelerating quickly to break away in an attempt to open up a gap ahead of the peloton, the main pack of riders. The hierarchy is fluid and may even change during a race, depending on whether the team is going for an overall win or just a stage win and how well the riders are going. And some of the rankings double up, e.g. a rouleur may also be a super-domestique.

A TYPICAL TOUR TEAM

Team leader
The rider deemed to have the best chance of winning overall. Usually a good climber and time triallist.

Super-domestique (aka lieutenant)
A rider who remains with the team leader for as long as possible during challenging stages.

Sprinter
A rider who is good at sprinting (fast acceleration over short periods). May be allowed to go alone for a stage win on flat stages. Some teams are based around a sprinter, so they are also the team leader.

Rouleur (a good all-rounder)
A strong, powerful rider, good on flat sections (may also be a super-domestique).

Lead-out rider
A rider who is good at sprinting, but who may not have the explosive power of the best sprinter in the team. They aim to get the best sprinter into a position near the finish line.

To win a stage: about 3 km before the finish, a lead-out train is formed by a line of four to five riders with the best sprinter at the back. The leading rider in the train cycles as fast as possible, then peels off when tired to let the next rider do the same, etc. until the best sprinter is left to go for the finish line.

Grimpeur ('climber')

A rider who is good at ascents (mountains!). The grimpeur may be allowed to go alone for a stage win on mountain stages, but may also be asked to be a lead-out rider for the team leader on similar stages.

Domestique ('servant')

He supports the team through tactics (forming or chasing down breakaways and attacks). The domestique creates a slipstream for the team leader and obtains water/food from the support vehicle for the rest of his teammates en route, like a superfast waiter!

THE FAMOUS TOUR JERSEYS

The jerseys are awarded to the leading riders in each category up to that point in the race, so the riders wearing them can change daily.

Maillot jaune (yellow jersey)

The prized yellow jersey is worn by the leader, the rider who has the lowest time overall in the race so far.

Maillot vert (green jersey)

Earned by the rider who has the most sprint points – points are awarded per day to the first riders across the line on the stage sprints and for time trials at certain sections along the route.

Maillot à pois (polka dot jersey, white with red dots)

The 'king of the mountains' wears this distinctive jersey for having earned the most points in the climbing stages.

Maillot blanc (white jersey)

Worn by the rider under twenty-five years of age with the lowest time overall at that point.

OTHER AWARDS

White-on-red identification number (instead of black-on-white)
The rider with the most 'fighting spirit' points – earned for attacking moves.

Yellow number (instead of white)
Awarded to the leading team, based on the lowest total time of the first three riders in each team.

Rainbow jersey (band of coloured horizontal stripes across a white background)
Worn by the world champion in a particular race discipline (time trial, sprint, etc.) – not specific to the Tour de France.

Unofficial award
The 'Lanterne Rouge' ('red light') is the last rider to complete the race. Just completing the Tour de France is a huge achievement so although the long list of runners-up is soon forgotten, the very last rider is often remembered.

The art of racing open-wheeled single-seater cars is governed by the FIA (Federation Internationale de l'Automobile) and named after the FIA's 'formulae' or rules that the cars and race teams must comply with. The FIA tinkers with the detail each season, to keep everyone, spectators included, on their toes. The FIA's global pathway is designed to allow the best drivers to progress from karting through F4, F3 and F2 to compete in the F1 World Championship, without being distracted by other championship series along the way.

Formula One

Inaugurated in 1950, the jewel in the Formula crown, the fastest road-course racing cars compete in the most glamorous and well known of all motorsport races. The cars are made by a handful of different manufacturers and must comply with the strict technical specifications. New circuits have been added over recent years but changes may be expected after new owners Liberty Media took over in 2017.

Formula Two

Replaced in 1985 by Formula 3000, F2 had a brief revival in 2009, was discontinued again in 2012, but made a comeback in 2017 when the FIA and the former GP2 series organisation agreed to create 'the ultimate training ground' for F1 in a new FIA F2 championship.

European Formula 3

Inaugurated in 1966, all Formula 3 cars must be stock block (built from a production model) with 2-litre engines built by different manufacturers.

Formula 4

For drivers aged fifteen and over and launched in 2014, F4 aims to keep things low-cost to help young drivers take their first step up from karting. Drivers race in national and regional championships.

GP series

Conceived by former F1 CEO Bernie Ecclestone and Flavio Briatore, the GP2 series was introduced in 2005 after the discontinuation of the FIA's feeder series Formula 3000, and the GP3 series was launched in 2010. Many champion drivers serve their apprenticeship with GP2.

Priority at Sea

The International Regulations for Preventing Collisions at Sea (aka COLREGS), based on a British system dating from 1862, have been adopted by most maritime states. This order of priority, designed to prevent a sea-going Mexican standoff, is determined by the vessels' function at the time of the meeting and by their position with relation to each other, and applies only when each has physical sight of the other (radar or sound signals are therefore excluded). The function of a boat is always contingent, so a fishing vessel is only a fishing vessel when its nets are out; on its way back to port, for example, it is classed merely as a power-driven vessel.

No vessel has absolute 'right of way' and the rules apply anywhere at sea but may be subject to local by-laws. A 'stand on' vessel maintains course and speed, proceeding unhindered, and a 'give way' vessel manoeuvres to keep clear. Deciding which vessel is which depends upon a wide range of factors, including each boat's method of propulsion, its position relative to the wind, its capability to manoeuvre and even its particular function at the time.

Not Under Command (NUC)
A vessel that is unable to manoeuvre and keep out of the way of other vessels due to exceptional circumstances, such as engine failure.

Restricted in Ability to Manoeuvre (RAM)
A vessel that, due to the nature of her work (e.g. dredging, laying cables), is less able to manoeuvre and keep out of the way of other vessels.

Constrained by Draft (CBD)
A power-driven vessel that is restricted in her ability to manoeuvre due to her draft (distance between the waterline and the bottom of a boat's hull) in relation to the available depth and width of navigable water.

Fishing vessels
Vessels engaged in fishing.

Vessels powered by sail
From dinghies to ocean-going super yachts.

Power-driven vessels
Includes sailboats under power.

EXCEPTIONS

Under sail
Port tack boats must give way to starboard tack.

Boats on the same tack – the boat to windward must take evasive action.

Motor-driven
Boats meeting head on – both turn to starboard. Make a sound signal – one short blast.

Two power-driven vessels crossing – the boat which has the other on her starboard side shall keep out of the way.

KNOTTY SUBJECT
In open water overtaking may be carried out either to port or to starboard, providing proper notice has been given (sound signals) and the boat to be overtaken has consented and taken appropriate measures. In a narrow channel, overtaking is usually carried out on the port side, if absolutely necessary, the rule as ever is good seamanship and common sense.

The Civil Aviation Authority's (CAA) Manual of Air Traffic Services issues a priority listing to guide air traffic controllers working in UK airspace. Category A is the highest priority rating.

Category A
Aircraft with an emergency (e.g. mechanical failure, crucial fuel shortage, seriously ill passenger).

Aircraft that has declared a 'Police Emergency'.

Ambulance aircraft when the safety of life is involved.

Category B
Aircraft operating search and rescue or other humanitarian missions.

Post-accident flight checks.

Other flights, including CAA-authorised Open Skies Flights. (The Open Skies Treaty permits 'mutual aerial observation'. Those states that are signatory to the treaty may conduct reconnaissance flights over the territory of other signatory states to collect information on military forces and activities.)

Category C
Flights carrying members of the British royal family.

Flights carrying visiting heads of state notified by NOTAM/ Temporary Supplement (i.e. an official notification).

Category D
Flights carrying heads of government or very senior government ministers notified by the CAA.

Category E
Flight check aircraft on or in transit to time or weather critical calibration flights.
Other flights authorised by the CAA.

Normal flights
Flights that have filed a flight plan in the normal way and conform with normal routing procedures.

Initial instrument flight tests conducted by the CAA Flight Examining Unit.

Category Z
Training, non-standard and other flights.

95

Olympian Gods

The Greeks had a god or goddess for every natural phenomenon, abstract concept and human emotion. They were ruled by the Olympian gods, who were led by the king and queen, Zeus and Hera. The Olympians descended from the Titans, who in turn descended from the primordial gods, born of original Chaos. Each generation fought the elder for power – Cronus fought and killed his father Ouranos, Zeus fought and killed his father Cronus. The fight between the Titans and the Olympians went on for ten years until Zeus prevailed and established his twelve-god pantheon on Mount Olympus.

1 PRIMORDIAL GODS BORN FROM CHAOS
Aether, Ananke, Chronos, Erebos, Eros, Gaia, Hemera, Hydros, Neboi, Nyx, Ouranos, Ourea, Phanes, Phusis, Pontus, Tartarus, Thalassa

Gaia (Earth) and **Ouranos** (sky) produced the Titans.

2 THE TITANS
Coeus, Crius, Cronus, Hyperion, Iapetus, Mnemosyne, Oceanus, Phoebe, Rhea, Tethys, Thea, Themis

Cronus (king of the Titans, god of devouring time) and **Rhea** (queen of heaven, goddess of female fertility and generation) produced the first generation of Olympian Gods.

3 THE OLYMPIAN GODS

Zeus, Hera, Demeter (goddess of agriculture), Poseidon (god of the sea and horses), Hades* (god of the underworld), Hestia** (goddess of hearth and home)

Zeus (god of the sky, king of the gods) and **Hera** (goddess of the female principle, queen of the gods) together and separately, produced the second generation.

Ares (god of war) son of Zeus and Hera.

Apollo (god of prophecy, oracles and music) son of Zeus and the Titaness Leto, twin to Artemis.

Artemis (goddess of the hunt and childbirth) daughter of Zeus and Leto, twin to Apollo.

Aphrodite (goddess of love and desire) daughter of Zeus and Dione OR created from sea foam.

Athena (goddess of wisdom and war) daughter of Zeus and **Metis** (daughter of Oceanus), born fully formed and armed from Zeus' head.

Hephaistos/Hephaestus (god of fire, smiths and metalcraft) son of Hera.

Hermes (god of roads and travel, communication and thievery, messenger of the gods) son of Zeus and the star nymph Maia.

Dionysos/Dionysus (god of altered states) son of Zeus and the mortal Theban princess Semele, born from Zeus' thigh.

* Hades was not an Olympian resident as he had his own realm below the Earth.

** Hestia later replaced by Dionysus as one of the twelve while remaining one of the lesser Olympians.

HESIOD'S GENEALOGY

Most of what we know about Greek gods comes from The Theogony ('The Genealogy of the Gods') by the poet Hesiod (eighth–seventh century BC). It is an aggregation of all the contemporary local traditions, expressed in a narrative poem.

96

Putting the Norse Gods in their Place

The Norse gods comprised three clans: the Aesir, the Vanir and the Jötun. After a protracted war between the Aesir and the Vanir, in which the Aesir were dominant, a truce was called, and hostages exchanged to ensure continued cooperation. The Aesir built Asgard, where they and their Vanir hostages lived. It was part of Midgard, the earthly realm in Norse mythology, linked to humanity by the rainbow bridge Bifröst. The remaining Vanir stayed in Vanaheim, and the Jötun, a race of giants, remained apart in Jötunheim although Odin and Thor had liaisons with several giantesses.

THE GODS OF ASGARD

MAJOR AESIR GODS	**Odin,** Allfather, Father of the gods. **Frigg,** wife of Odin, queen of Asgard.
SONS OF ODIN	**Thor,** son of Frigg and Odin; god of the sky and thunder. **Baldur,** son of Frigg and Odin; god of light, innocence and beauty. **Vidar,** son of Odin and giantess Grid; god of vengeance. **Vali,** son of Odin and the giantess Rind, born to avenge his brother Baldur.

OTHER MAJOR GODS	**Bragi**, husband to Idun, possible son of Odin; god of poetry.
	Idun, wife of Bragi; goddess of youth and immortality.
	Loki, son of the giant Farbáuti, foster brother of Odin; trickster god.
	Hel, daughter of Loki; queen of the underworld.
	Heimdall, guardian of Asgard; possibly a son of Odin.
	Týr, god of combat and glory, son of the giant Hymir (or possibly Odin).
VANIR HOSTAGES	**Njord**, god of the sea.
	Freyr, son of Njord; god of fertility.
	Freya, daughter of Njord, twin to Freyr; goddess of love, beauty, death and war.
MINOR AESIR GODS	**Sif**, wife of Thor, mother of the valkyrie Thrud, Ull and Modi.
	Forseti, son of Baldur and Nanna; god of truth, peace and justice.
	Ull, son of Sif, step-son of Thor; god of hunting.
	Hermod, son or servant of Odin; messenger of gods.
	Hoenir, god of prophesy.
	Hod, son of Odin, brother of Baldur; god of darkness.
	Meili, son of Odin, brother of Thor.
	Modi, the Angry, son of Thor and Sif.
	Magni, the Strong, son of Thor and the giantess Járnsaxa.
	Nanna, daughter of Nep, wife of Baldur.
	Vili and Vé, brothers of Odin; co-creators of first humans Askr and Embla.

MIGHTY MARVELLOUS

Thor (and his mighty hammer Mjöllnir) and Loki lead other lives as fictional superheroes in the Marvel Comic universe. And J. R. R. Tolkien famously drew some of his inspiration from Norse mythology for his Lord of the Rings *saga.*

97

Demons

Demons weren't always considered a bad thing – in ancient Greek belief, a 'daemon' was a lesser divinity or supernatural being, positioned, along with heroes and angels, somewhere between gods and humans. The Catholic Church, however, believes a demon to be a fallen angel under the command of Lucifer, and destined to remain a demon for ever, because once a spiritual being has turned away from God, it cannot turn back. However, each demon is said to have an opposing saint in heaven, whose actions can negate those of the demon.

The sixteenth-century German bishop and theologian Peter Binsfeld proposed that seven of the demons – the seven Princes of Hell – tempt mankind to commit the traditional seven deadly sins. The offending demons are presented here in decreasing order of severity of their associated sins according to Dante's *Divine Comedy* (see page 92) completed in 1320.

Lucifer (Sin: Pride)

The Emperor of Hell, who led a rebellion against God and as punishment was cast down from Heaven by the Archangel Michael, protector of the Church Militant. Lucifer is derived from the Latin *lux* ('light') + *fer* ('bearing'). Luciferianism is a belief system whose followers regard Lucifer as the bringer of light and wisdom.

Leviathan (Sin: Envy)

The Grand Admiral of Hell, portrayed as a great whale-like sea monster, with the gates of hell in his mouth. His description in the Book of Job depicts an alarming creature: 'His sneezes flash forth light', 'His breath kindles coals' and 'His underparts are like sharp potsherds'.

Amon (Sin: Wrath)

The Grand Marquis of Hell, who promotes hate and anger in the human heart. One of the lesser-known demons, Amon is depicted as a fire-breathing wolf with a serpent's tail, or as a man with a raven's head.

Belphegor (Sin: Sloth)

The Prince of Hell, portrayed as a horned demon (or sometimes an attractive young woman), who tempts the slothful with ideas for inventions that will bring them riches. Belphegor is said to be Hell's ambassador to France, and to haunt the Louvre in Paris.

Mammon (Sin: Greed)

From the Aramaic *māmōn*, meaning 'riches', Mammon is not so much a demon as a concept, although he is portrayed as a fallen angel in Milton's epic poem *Paradise Lost*, published in 1667. Mammon has come to be defined as 'wealth regarded as a false object of worship': 'Ye cannot serve God and Mammon.'

Beelzebub (Sin: Gluttony)

The Prince of Demons, whose name translates from Hebrew as 'Lord of the Flies'. According to the Testament of Solomon, he entertained himself with activities such as bringing about destruction by means of tyrants, causing demons to be worshipped and provoking jealousy and murder.

Asmodeus (Sin: Lust)

The King of Hell, who delights in destroying marriages – killing off seven husbands of Sarah, the daughter of Raguel, the Angel of Justice, before being driven away, repelled by the odour of smoked fish liver. He is described as having three heads (the crowned head of a man, flanked by a bull and a ram), a serpent's tail, the feet of a goose, and flaming breath.

A FALL FROM GRACE

According to the French inquisitor Sébastien Michaelis'
1613 classification (revealed to him, surprisingly, by a
demon), demons belong to the corresponding choir of
angels from which they fell. Four of the above demons –
Lucifer, Leviathan, Beelzebub and Asmodeus – are said to
have belonged to the highest of the nine celestial orders,
Seraphim.

Dionysus' Hierarchy of Angels

After studying references to angels in the Scriptures and other sources, Pseudo-Dionysius the Areopagite, thought to have been a Syrian monk who lived around 500 AD, compiled this hierarchy, which is still used today.

FIRST SPHERE

1 SERAPHIM
'The burning ones' since they are closest to God and radiate pure light. Often depicted with six wings, Seraphim glorify and praise God.

2 CHERUBIM
Originally depicted with four wings and four faces, they guard the gates of Eden. Today they are portrayed as cherubic babies with wings.

3 THRONES
They contemplate God's will in order to carry out His decisions.

SECOND SPHERE

4 DOMINIONS
They carry out God's wishes and regulate the other angels.

5 VIRTUES
They encourage people to trust in God, often performing miracles to inspire this trust. The Virtues are associated with acts of heroism and help strengthen courage.

6 POWERS
The Powers are viewed as the angels of birth and death. They also prevent the 'fallen angels' from taking control and help humans overcome temptation.

THIRD SPHERE

7 PRINCIPALITIES
They protect against the invasion of evil angels and are the guardian angels of nations and rulers.

8 ARCHANGELS
They deliver God's messages to humans and command His 'armies' of angels in the battle with the 'sons of darkness'.

9 ANGELS
The angels closest to humans, they are intermediaries between God and people. They pray for and guide humans.

The Academic Hierarchy of the Genres

In the seventeenth century, the great European academies in Rome, Paris and London established a hierarchy for painting that held sway for two centuries. André Félibien des Avaux, consultant to the French Académie Royale de Peinture et de Sculpture (Royal Academy of Painting and Sculpture), which held a central role in academic art, first announced the rankings in 1669. They were based on the belief in the Italian Renaissance that the highest form of art was the representation of the human form.

Man was the measure of all things and the moral force of each genre played a key role. Size mattered too, with the display value of each genre contributing to its place in the hierarchy. Still life ranked lowest, with the human figure performing acts of legendary or allegorical significance at the pinnacle, often nude or partially nude as this was believed to demand the greatest artistic skill. The impressive scale of history painting meant such pieces were suitable for public spaces, galleries and churches, and for large canvases, whereas the smaller size of still-life canvases made them more appropriate for domestic viewing. The top-down hierarchy was as follows:

1 History Painting (grand genre)
Large-scale narrative paintings of historical, classical, religious, mythological and allegorical scenes. Heroic and noble deeds were portrayed and moral messages conveyed for the edification of the viewer.

2 Portraiture or Portrait Painting
Scenes of heroic individuals, often larger than life, intended for public viewing, but also private portraiture.

3 Genre Painting (scènes de genre)
Small-scale scenes of everyday life with ordinary people.

4 Landscapes
Scenic views of the countryside, seas, rivers, mountains and towns. The seventeenth-century Dutch art historian Samuel van Hoogstraten called landscapists 'the common footmen in the army of art'.

5 Still Life
Arrangements of flowers, fruit, food and everyday objects.

100   The Orchestra

Today's orchestra comprises four instrument families: strings (violins, violas, cellos, double basses), woodwind (flutes, oboes, clarinets, bassoons), brass (trumpets, trombones, tuba, French horns) and percussion (timpani, cymbals, triangle, xylophone...).

At the helm is the conductor (sometimes addressed as maestro), who sets the tempo, ensures the entry of various instruments in the score and shapes the music. Each section has its own leader.

STRINGS

First violins (primo)
Principal first violin – also orchestra leader/concert master.
Assistant concert master (replaces first violin in their absence, or there are two leaders).
Additional first violins – numbers vary, usually seated two to a stand/desk (hence 'sitting second, third, fourth desk'); the player on the left generally turns the page.

Second violins (secondo)
(Usually play in lower registers than the first violins.)
Principal second violin.
Additional second violins – numbers vary, seating as above.

The leader of the first violin section is the spokesperson for the rest of the orchestra and is second-in-command to the conductor, and as his or her right-hand (wo)man is usually seated to the conductor's left. He/she is the first point of contact between the conductor and the orchestra and liaises between the orchestra and its management. In the Baroque era orchestras were often led by the concert master.

Other sections
Each string section also has a principal player and follows the desk/stand system. There are principals, co-principals, associate principals and sub-principals within a section and the number depends on the size of the section and on the size and wealth of the orchestra. Other instrumental groups also generally have a principal. The orchestra is, however, an essentially democratic body.

PIANO

The piano is a solo instrument and not part of the general orchestra. It is brought on stage for a particular piece and its position is determined by the conductor, who can also decide the seating arrangements for the entire orchestra.

CONTEMPORARY SYMPHONY ORCHESTRA
The composition of today's symphony orchestra remains much as it was in the late nineteenth century, with typically thirty violins, twelve violas, ten cellos, eight double basses, four of each woodwind, eight horns, four trumpets, three trombones, one tuba and several percussion instruments. Numbers vary according to the piece being played and the demands of the score. For example, Shostakovich's Fourth Symphony requires six flutes.

101

The Ballet Company

Most classical ballet companies have a hierarchy, but structure and rigidity, and job titles, vary between companies and countries. Early ballet companies such as the Paris Opera Ballet and the Mariinsky Ballet in St Petersburg, Russia, established a basic structure of seniority, which has evolved in different ways in companies around the world. Different hierarchies for male and female dancers have now merged into a gender-neutral classification. In the nineteenth and very early twentieth centuries some companies revolved around a single star ballerina but rosters today include several principal dancers. Some appoint a Principal Guest Artist – Sylvie Guillem and Carlos Acosta both held this title with the Royal Ballet in London. Smaller companies, unfettered by the constraints of boards of directors or government funding requirements, can devise their own structure to suit their repertoire and size. Some are completely egalitarian and all the dancers are named as part of the group.

ABSOLUTELY EXCEPTIONAL
The term 'Prima Ballerina Assoluta' is an exceptional title awarded to a ballerina who has been an integral part of a company's success. Margot Fonteyn was Prima Ballerina Assoluta at the Royal Ballet and to date remains the only dancer to be awarded the honour by the company.

In major companies in the UK and Europe, the structure might be:

Artistic Director
Often a retired dancer, he or she makes casting decisions, schedules programmes, commissions choreographers (and may also choreograph themselves), and hires and fires dancers. In major companies the Artistic Director reports to a board of governors, and, ultimately, to the government minister or official in charge of arts and culture.

Assistant Artistic Director
Supports the Artistic Director and monitors rehearsals and standards.

Ballet masters and repetiteurs
Usually give the daily classes and direct rehearsals. Repetiteurs are responsible for coaching dancers in individual roles and for ensuring that the choreographer's intentions are adhered to.

Dancers

Principal dancers
The highest rank within the company, they usually appear in leading roles (e.g. Aurora and the Prince in *The Sleeping Beauty*). In the Paris Opera Ballet they are known as *danseur étoile* (literally 'star dancer').

Principal character artists
Dancers who perform important character roles in a ballet.

First soloists & soloists
Dancers who perform solo and minor roles (e.g. the Lilac Fairy in *The Sleeping Beauty*) and can also understudy the principal role.

First artists or coryphées
The more senior members of the corps de ballet.

Corps de ballet ('body of the ballet')
Comprises male and female dancers who dance as an ensemble, as one 'body', with synchronised movements. There is also a ranking structure within the corps de ballet, usually based on the length of service (first year corps, second year corps, and so on).

In the USA, major companies are usually structured as follows:

Principal dancers

Soloists

Corps de ballet

Apprentices
Apprentices are usually young dancers straight out of school, who are hired on a yearly or seasonal basis so that the artistic staff can watch how they develop.

In Russia the structure is usually:

Principal dancers

Leading soloists

First soloists

Soloists

Coryphées

Corps de ballet

Large Russian companies also have a parallel company of character dancers.

102

Music Sales

In February 1942, the American record label RCA Victor awarded Glenn Miller and His Orchestra a gold record to celebrate the sale of 1.2 million copies of the still instantly recognisable song 'Chattanooga Choo Choo', starting a music sales success ranking that is still going strong today. Certification originally related to sales of a physical single or album, but now, with the advent of new technology, there are also awards for sales of digital downloads and even phone ringtones.

UNITED STATES

In the USA, sales awards are certified by the Recording Industry Association of America (RIAA). The criteria in terms of numbers of physical albums and downloads sold are currently:

Albums
Gold: 500,000 copies

Platinum: 1 million copies

Multi-platinum: More than 2 million

Diamond: More than 10 million

Downloads
Gold: 100,000

Platinum: 200,000

Multi-platinum: 400,000 then increments of 200,000

THRILLING FIGURES
Michael Jackson's 1982 album Thriller *holds the Guinness World Record for the world's best-selling album, and has been certified twenty-nine times platinum by the RIAA. It shares the title of best-selling album in the USA with the Eagles'* Their Greatest Hits.

UNITED KINGDOM

In the UK, sales awards are certified by the British Phonographic Industry. The criteria in terms of numbers of albums sold* are currently:

Silver: 60,000

Gold: 100,000

Platinum: 300,000

Multi-platinum: Multiples of 300,000

*1,000 streams count as equivalent to 1 album sale

QUEEN OF HITS
In July 2016, the UK's Official Albums Chart celebrated its sixtieth birthday and confirmed Queen's 1981 album Greatest Hits *as the nation's best-seller to date, having sold over six million copies in the UK.*

CANADA

Achieving a sales award from Music Canada appears less challenging than in the neighbouring United States – but its population is only 10 per cent of that of the USA, which is reflected in the criteria for certification, currently:

Albums

Gold: 40,000

Platinum: 80,000

Diamond: 800,000

Double diamond: 1,600,000

Ringtones

Gold: 20,000

Platinum: 40,000

Diamond: 400,000

Double diamond: 800,000

The best-selling album worldwide by a Canadian artist is Shania Twain's *Come On Over*, at thirty-nine million copies.

FRANCE

Best-selling French artists are recognised by the Syndicat National de l'édition Phonographique. If the following sales criteria seem outrageously harsh, it's because in 2016 France adopted a new system of awards based on converting sales into stream equivalents, instead of the reverse system used by other countries:

Gold: 10,000,000

Platinum: 20,000,000

Diamond: 35,000,000

STREAMING AHEAD

An early beneficiary of the new system was the French singer-songwriter Vianney, who released an album in November 2016 and just over one month later achieved a double platinum certification.

Films are rated by the Motion Picture Association of America (MPAA). The ratings have no legal force, and film makers have no obligation to have their film rated before it is released. States can apply their own laws. Films are rated for violence, language, substance abuse, nudity and sex. The system is regulated by the Classification and Rating Administration (CARA). The MPAA also rates trailers and advertising material. TV and video games are rated by other bodies.

These are the current ratings, as established in the 1990s.

G (General Audience)
Suitable for all ages.

PG (Parental Guidance Suggested)
Some material may not be suitable for children.

PG13 (Parental Guidance Strongly Cautioned)
Some material may not be suitable for children under 13.

R (Restricted)
Children under 17 need an accompanying parent or adult guardian.

NC-17 (Adults only)
No one aged 17 or under.

NR (Not rated)
Films that have not been submitted for rating.

UR (Unrated)
Films that have not been submitted, or uncut, recut or extended versions of films that may have been rated.

Trailers and advertising material

Green – when the trailer accompanies a similarly rated film.

Yellow – for films on the internet only, rated PG13 or stronger.

Red – the trailer is restricted, suitable for previewing R and NC-17 films only.

This Film Has Not Been Rated – displayed in trailers if the film is unrated.

104

British Film Classification

In the UK, films and videos/DVD material are rated for suitability by age by the British Board of Film Classification. They follow agreed guidelines which are revised regularly to match changing social norms and mores. The board has no statutory powers, however; these remain with local councils who have the ultimate say in licensing films to be shown in cinemas.

In each age group, examiners consider what the film contains or presents in terms of

- discrimination, discriminatory language or behaviour
- drugs
- imitable behaviour (including mention, sight or use of weapons)
- language
- nudity
- sex
- threat (horror)
- violence

They also consider the overall tone and impact (how it makes the audience feel), genre, context and format since DVDs for home viewing may be seen by underage viewers.

FILM AND FUNCTION
The film industry set up the British Board of Film Censors in 1912 as an independent body to bring a degree of uniformity to the classification of film nationally. The name was changed to the British Board of Film Classification in 1984, to better represent its function.

U
Suitable for all over the age of four.

PG Parental Guidance
Usually suitable for eight years and upwards, but it is the parent's responsibility to decide if their child is particularly sensitive.

12A

A cinema release suitable for twelve years and over. Children under twelve may watch 12A movies providing they have an accompanying adult.

12

Video release suitable for twelve years and over.
Children under twelve may not buy or view 12-rated videos.

15

Suitable for fifteen years and over.

18

Suitable only for adults.

R18

Suitable for adults on licensed premises only. This category is mostly pornography; works containing a lot of very strong sexual imagery. Strong fetish material is usually rated R18.

A DIFFERENCE OF OPINION

In the UK, the film version of the novel Fifty Shades of Grey, *with its sexual content, was given an '18' rating whereas the French classification board, the CNC, said it 'would not shock a lot of people' and gave it a '12' rating. The Malaysian Film Censorship Board banned it completely whereas in the USA it was given an R rating (age 17 and under must be accompanied by an adult).*

Golf has a partly bird-themed hierachy to denote how well or otherwise a player performs in relation to the par rating of a hole (usually, eighteen holes per golf course). Unusually, this hierarchy extends both upwards and downwards from a centre point – par.

DEEP DESPAIR

Triple bogey – three strokes above par

Double bogey – two strokes above par

Bogey – one stroke above par (e.g. a score of four on a par-three hole)

Par – the number of strokes a scratch player (expert, handicap zero) normally requires to complete the hole

Birdie – one stroke under par (birdie = 'awesome' in early twentieth-century American slang)

Eagle – two strokes under par

Albatross – three strokes under par (British)/double eagle (American)

UTTER EUPHORIA

Condor – four under par (unofficial and extremely rare, e.g. a hole-in-one on a par-five hole, drinks all round at the nineteenth hole or clubhouse)

HANDICAPS

The handicap system enables all golfers to compete on equal terms, no matter what their level of ability. Here is the CONGU® Council of National Golf Unions' system used in Britain and Ireland (handicaps with a decimal place have been rounded up or down); some other countries have different rules for calculating handicap.

Category 1 Handicaps of five or below (the best players)

Category 2 Handicaps of six to twelve inclusive

Category 3 Handicaps of thirteen to twenty inclusive

Category 4 Handicaps of twenty-one to twenty-eight inclusive

Category 5 Handicaps of twenty-nine to thirty-six inclusive (Ladies Only)

Juniors' Handicaps of twenty-nine to fifty-four

Snooker Balls

Snooker is played with one white cue ball, fifteen red balls, and one ball each of six other colours: yellow, green, brown, blue, pink and black. Balls must be potted alternately red and a colour until there are no reds left. Up to that point, coloured balls that have been potted are replaced on the table. Once there are no reds, the coloured balls must be potted in ascending order of their value to finish the game. Black is the last to be potted.

red	1 point
yellow	2 points
green	3 points
brown	4 points
blue	5 points
pink	6 points
black	7 points

SNOOKERED
To snooker means to prevent your opponent from making a clear shot at their target by strategically positioning the balls thanks to some smart play on your part.

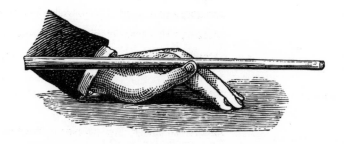

The English Men's Football League

English men's football teams are organised into a pyramid of interconnected leagues. It is based on a system of promotion and relegation that depends on points gathered throughout a season. Theoretically any team can climb to the top, or sink down to the bottom.

There are more than 140 football leagues in England but the top eleven are the most significant. The first is the self-governing Premier League, established in 1992 by a breakaway group of the top teams of what was then the First Division. The English Football League (established 1888) runs levels two, three and four. The National League System (NLS), answerable to the Football Association (FA), runs levels five to eleven.

Premier League

Level One
The Premier League
Twenty clubs
Nationwide
Full-time professional
Self-funding corporation, not sponsored

English Football League

Level Two
The English Football League: the Championship
Twenty-four clubs
Nationwide
Full-time professional
Commercially sponsored

Level Three
The English Football League: League One
Twenty-four clubs
Nationwide
Full-time professional
Commercially sponsored

Level Four
The English Football League: League Two
Twenty-four clubs
Nationwide
Full-time professional
Commercially sponsored

National League

Level Five
National League
Twenty-four clubs
Nationwide
Professional and semi-professional
Commercially sponsored

Level Six
(All Level Six leagues are of equal status)
National League North
Twenty-two clubs
Regional
Professional and semi-professional
Commercially sponsored

Level Six
National League South
Twenty-two clubs
Regional
Professional and semi-professional
Commercially sponsored

Level Seven
(All Level Seven leagues are of equal status)
Northern Premier League
North of England and North Wales
Premier Division
Twenty-four clubs
Semi-professional and amateur
Commercially sponsored

Level Seven
Southern Football League
Midlands, South and South-West England, South Wales
Premier Division
Twenty-four clubs
Semi-professional and amateur
Commercially sponsored

Level Seven
Isthmian League
London and South-East England
Premier Division
Twenty-four clubs
Semi-professional and amateur
Commercially sponsored

Level Eight
(All Level Eight leagues are of equal status)
Northern Premier League
North of England and North Wales
Division One North
Twenty-two clubs
Semi-professional and amateur
Commercially sponsored

Level Eight
Northern Premier League
North of England and North Wales
Division One South
Twenty-two clubs
Semi-professional and amateur
Commercially sponsored

Level Eight
Southern Football League
Midlands, South and South-West England, South Wales
Division One Central
Twenty-two clubs
Semi-professional and amateur
Commercially sponsored

Level Eight
Southern Football League
Midlands, South and South-West England, South Wales
Division One South & West
Twenty-two clubs
Semi-professional and amateur
Commercially sponsored

Level Eight
Isthmian League
London and South-East England
Division One North
Twenty-four clubs
Semi-professional and amateur

Level Eight
Isthmian League
London and South-East England
Division One South
Twenty-four clubs
Semi-professional and amateur

Level Nine
Top divisions from fourteen leagues round the country
in parallel
Nineteen to twenty-three clubs per division
Semi-professional and amateur

Level Ten
First divisions, with some premier divisions, from
seventeen leagues around the country in parallel
Fourteen to twenty-two clubs per division
Semi-professional and amateur

Level Eleven
First divisions, with some premier divisions, from
forty-three leagues around the country in parallel
Fourteen to twenty clubs per division
Semi-professional and amateur

LEAGUE AND NON-LEAGUE
*Confusingly, the National League System clubs are known
as non-league, because they were not part of the original
English Football League.*

The game begins with two 'armies' of sixteen chess pieces facing each other across the board in order of ascending rank. Each piece is assigned a point value, which does not affect the game but allows players to evaluate the risk of loss. The aim is to trap your opponent's king in 'checkmate', so that it cannot escape by moving, blocking or capturing your threatening piece. Game over.

So that the moves can be recorded, each of the sixty-four squares on the board has a grid number. The eight squares across the board run from A to H, from left to right. The squares down the board run from 1 to 8, from bottom to top. The board is set up so that for each player, the bottom far right corner contains a white square. The pieces in order of value are:

King
Starting place on board: fourth in from the right in the back row always on a square of opposite colour (e8 black king; e1 white king).
Value: priceless.
Moves: only one square, but in any direction (forwards, backwards, sideways, diagonally).
Illegal moves: the king must not put himself in check.

Queen

Starting place on board: fourth in from the left in the back row, always on a square of the same colour as herself (d8 black queen, d1 white queen).

Value: nine points.

Moves: as far as wanted in a straight line forwards, backwards, sideways, diagonally; if she captures a piece, the move is over.

Illegal moves: the queen may not move through her own pieces.

Rook

Starting place on board: the two rooks stand at either end of the back row (a8 and h8 black rooks, a1 and h1 white rooks).

Value: five points.

Moves: as far as wanted forwards, backwards and sideways.

Bishop

Starting place on board: one each side of the king and queen in the back row (c8 and f8 black; c1 and f1 white).

Value: three points.

Moves: as far as wanted diagonally only; must always stay on the colour on which it began.

Knight

Starting place on board: one each side of each bishop in the back row (b8 and g8 black; b1 and g1 white).

Value: three points.

Moves: in an L shape, two squares in one direction, and then one at a 90 degree angle; the only piece that can move over other pieces.

Pawn

Starting place on board: eight pawns, one in each square of the second row (a7–h7 black, a2–h2 white).

Value: one point.

Moves: forwards or backwards, two squares on the first move, one square per move after that; can only take pieces diagonally in front of them.

Additional powers: if a pawn makes it to the opposing back row, it can redeem any one of its side's pieces that have been captured; this is how a captured queen can be rescued.

Index